George

ff

faber and faber

LONDON · BOSTON

This translation first published in 1997
by Faber and Faber Limited
3 Queen Square London WC1N 3AU

Typeset by Faber and Faber Ltd
Printed in England by Clays Ltd, St Ives plc

Translation © Faber & Faber, 1997

Originally published in French by Editions Ircam, 1996
© Editions Ircam, 1996

Music examples reproduced by kind permission of Faber Music Ltd

A CIP record for this book
is available from the British Library

ISBN 0-571-19151-7

10 9 8 7 6 5 4 3 2 1

Contents

Risto Nieminen is a former Artistic Director of
IRCAM, and is now the Director of the Helsinki
Music Festival.
Renaud Machart is a writer and music critic.
His most recent book, *Poulenc*, was published by
Editions du Seuil in 1995.

English translations by Julian Anderson and
Michael Durnin

Interview with George Benjamin

Risto Nieminen

Childhood

It was with the recorder, like many children, that I took my first musical steps at the age of five or six. My teacher, who also taught piano, thought that I had a talent for music. She told my parents, who then encouraged me to learn the piano. From the first few lessons, I adored and was fascinated by the instrument. Shortly after, I started to compose.

There weren't any musicians in my family, though my parents are very creative. They are meticulous in their work, details are very important to them, so maybe it's not surprising that I've found the same attitude always applying to my own endeavours.

When I was five or six, it was the age of the Beatles and I didn't like classical music; I refused even to listen to it. My love for it came shortly afterwards, when I was about seven, thanks to Walt Disney's *Fantasia*. That was a decisive moment. On my way home after seeing the film, I bought a record of Beethoven and then even threw all my 45s in the dustbin. From that moment on, I knew what I wanted to do: compose music. It was a total conversion. From then, from the ages of eight to ten, I was interested in only one thing, with the kind of crazy enthusiasm that a child might have for a football team, except that for me it was for Beethoven. I bought scores and records, and even wrote booklets, which I illustrated. I listened to his symphonies non-stop, and didn't like much other music. Afterwards my repertoire grew, thank goodness.

At school, the other children did not share my passion for music and I felt somewhat isolated. Happily, some teachers took me up, such as the rather terrifying Latin teacher who loved Bach, or the English master who introduced me to Berlioz, my second musical love. My relations with the school music teachers were unpredictable: there was often a tension, though some were very kind.

At the schools that I went to we did a lot of theatre. That was wonderful: Shakespeare, Ben Jonson, Bernard Shaw, and shows devised by the pupils. For these shows I wrote incidental music, preludes, songs, atmospheric music. I invited all of those who could to play my notes. I conducted ensembles consisting of out-of-tune pianos, four recorders, clarinet, guitar, trumpet, five percussionists. It was exciting, even if it wasn't well played, to hear what I had written. I also regularly went to concerts, once or twice a week, often with the score. I heard Klemperer conduct Mahler, Böhm Mozart, Karajan Beethoven, lots of great conductors and the whole repertoire. I heard dozens of performances of Mahler's second and ninth, *The Rite of Spring*, *Also Sprach Zarathustra*, *Symphonie Fantastique*, all the Beethoven symphonies. I was always seated high up so that I could see the orchestra more clearly.

I also started on modern music. I discovered Ligeti by seeing *2001, A Space Odyssey* in the cinema (an art form which remains crucial for me). The strange music from the film appealed to me, and I bought the enormous score of *Atmosphères* which, at the time, was bigger than me. I saw Henze conduct his compositions with the London Sinfonietta when I was fourteen. At school I heard music for organ that I found fascinating. I asked, 'What are these harmonies?' and for the first time I heard the name of Messiaen.

Certain teachers were helpful. *Wozzeck* was played in class. I thought it was like Mahler, pushed further. A real thrill! I caught Boulez on television when I was quite young, in a programme in which he talked about *Pli selon pli*. I saw him later on at the BBC Proms where he conducted Ligeti's *San Francisco Polyphony* and his own *Rituel*. Berio and Stockhausen were known names, and Birtwistle. I wasn't completely ignorant, but I wasn't completely *au courant* either.

Studies in Paris

Up to the age of sixteen, I didn't want a composition
teacher and really I didn't have one until Messiaen. I
thought it was something private, secret. But I had needed
a teacher to improve my piano technique and to teach me
generally about music. I had the luck to meet a wonderful
musician, Peter Gellhorn. He had left Germany for
England just before the war. His teacher had known
Brahms and he knew the whole repertoire, especially
German: Bach, Beethoven, Wagner . . . He became my
piano teacher when I was thirteen. He also looked at my
scores – he didn't say much, but he was very encouraging.

It was through Gellhorn that I met Messiaen. I had seen
in the Larousse Encyclopaedia a page on 'Messiaen and his
famous class at the Conservatoire, the greatest class in the
world, the centre of modern music'. A photo showed a
teacher surrounded by several students. And I thought that
if he was the best, the most important, I ought to try.
Gellhorn knew Messiaen: he had been the conductor of the
BBC Singers who had sung several of his works. Gellhorn
wrote a letter to Messiaen in which he said, I think (I've
never seen the letter), that I was an interesting student and
that he wanted to introduce me. It took several months to
get a reply since Messiaen was extremely busy. Then he
replied very kindly at the beginning of 1976, saying that he
would like to meet him with his pupil. We were delighted.
(Naïvely, I thought that every teacher in the world wrote
to Messiaen asking him to meet interesting students. Later,
I learned to my amazement that it was the only time it had
happened in his career as a teacher.)

It was only after he had written that I went to a concert
to hear *Turangalîla*. I was deeply impressed; I loved the
sound, but the lack of tension in the music troubled me. I
found Messiaen's music strange, far from my experience
and yet fascinating. But what a sound! It was then that I
had an intuition of what sort of teacher he would be. A

young student composer is lost: he doesn't know how to start, how to become a composer or what style to pursue. To know that there was someone to go to, someone of great strength, even if I didn't know his music very well, seemed to me a possible route.

When I arrived at Messiaen's flat in Paris with Gellhorn I was terrified. I had just turned sixteen and I thought my destiny was in his hands. He asked me to play one of my pieces on the piano. I was so nervous that I played it twice as fast as it should have been. A few seconds after playing, I turned to see his reaction. With a big smile he explained that although the harmonies were good I had played it much too fast. And then he whistled it at the right speed. That was that: instead of staying two hours we stayed together three hours, playing all my youthful pieces. He suggested that I become his pupil first of all as a guest, since I had to finish at school, and then to join his composition class and the piano class of his wife, Yvonne Loriod, at the Paris Conservatoire. I was so inspired by this meeting that I immediately started to compose my first really ambitious work, a sonata for violin and piano. The first movement, which was completed when I returned to Paris some months later, was an important evolution for me.

The first year, I sat in as a 'friend'. You can imagine how it felt for a sixteen-year-old English schoolboy to be invited by Messiaen 'as a friend'. For the first year, I went to Paris once a month, for two days, for two classes with Messiaen and one with Yvonne Loriod. So I was with Messiaen for eight or nine hours – amazingly long classes – and three or four hours with Loriod. It was almost the first time I had been abroad. At the same time I continued my studies at school. It was an incredible shock to go to Paris, to be beside this great composer and his other pupils, coming from all sorts of countries, many of whom were twice my age. Messiaen usually wanted me to sit beside him, to his right. He would often put questions to me, asking if I understood. It was like a light, there was a sort of joy in him, a profound love of music that he wanted to share with others.

The second year, I passed the exams to enter the Conservatoire in composition and piano. When school finished, I went to live in France. Three times a week I attended Messiaen's courses. We did an enormous amount of work on harmony. Each week, I played two hundred chords on the piano, and for an hour he would listen and criticize them. At home, I must have written hundreds of pages of chords, just chords. I remember particularly an extraordinary analysis of Debussy's *Pelléas et Mélisande* which lasted six weeks, going through it bar by bar. He also analyzed Stravinsky, Ravel, classical pieces, Stockhausen, Dutilleux, Lutosławski and Ligeti, Boulez, Xenakis and lots of his own pieces in detail, such as *Poèmes pour Mi*, *Chronochromie* and *La Transfiguration*. Several former students came to explain their works. Virtuoso instrumentalists demonstrated new playing techniques.

At this time, when I was seventeen, I met Pierre Boulez at the Conservatoire; he had come to conduct some student works with the Conservatoire orchestra. The son of his publisher, Thomas Schlee, my best friend in the class, introduced me very briefly. I went to premières by the Ensemble Intercontemporain and saw the construction of IRCAM. I went to huge numbers of concerts, at Radio France, the Conservatoire, all over Paris. I met Stockhausen and Xenakis with Messiaen.

I think I composed the first movement of the Piano Sonata during the summer and autumn of 1977. I played it to an examining board to enter the Conservatoire officially. Then I carried on with it very quickly when I was in Paris, about ten pages a week, which I would then play in Messiaen's class. He made criticisms and suggestions. The piece was really written right in front of him. I finished it in January or February and premièred it at Radio France. Messiaen came with Yvonne Loriod – their loyalty to their students was legendary. The piece is very virtuosic, though that's not why it was composed. Every time I played it, I broke a piano. When later I came to play it for a second time for Alexander Goehr he said, 'Don't touch my piano!' At the

Piano Sonata (extract). © 1978 Faber Music Ltd.
Reproduced by kind permission.

first London performance of the Sonata there was a broken string, blood on the keyboard, and a key even flew off into the audience. It's a beginner's piece, and I'm not particularly attached to it any more. It explores elements that Messiaen had taught me during that year, so I used techniques at the end that I didn't know about when I was writing the beginning. Still, there is a kind of tension in the piece which suggests the desire for continuity and development that has nothing to do with Messiaen.

During the last five or six months of working with Messiaen I was blocked, unable to compose. During this time, from the end of the sixties to the end of the seventies, to add to the normal difficulties of starting to compose – which are always there – European music was in a difficult situation. The dogma of Darmstadt had had its day, but the inhibiting rules remained; the creative need underlying the rules had disappeared and all that was left was the rigidity. For instance, when I played more consonant chords on the piano, other students at the Conservatoire made fun of me, the teachers too. They all found it funny, except for Messiaen, of course. I was strongly against Darmstadt music, though that may be because Messiaen never really explained well what serial music could do. Nowadays, I am less hostile but at that time I hated the sound of that music, its coldness, a sort of grey dissonance, a kind of static quality that I found horrible.

I wanted to do something else. I found a really original poetic and expressive power in Messiaen's harmonies, an element which I thought had been neglected. My first reaction was that contemporary music had no harmonic beauty, even the word 'harmony' was taboo. Messiaen was touched by that; it was a point of contact between us. Also, Messiaen's revolutionary rhythmic concepts interested me very much. When we first met, he thought that I was too primitive rhythmically and that I needed to develop. So, along with the harmony, I did a lot of research into rhythmic construction.

At Cambridge

I left Paris because Messiaen retired. The other tutors wanted me to stay to complete the composition course, but without Messiaen the Conservatoire wouldn't have been the same. So I decided to come back to this country and go to Cambridge. There I could digest all the material I had learned with Messiaen. I had time to reflect, to think, in relative isolation. At the same time I began to conduct classical and modern music with a student orchestra. I was able to play two Mozart piano concertos as soloist, and my own works started to be published, recorded and performed, even abroad, after *Ringed by the Flat Horizon* was played at the BBC Proms in August 1980.

I studied with Alexander Goehr, who had been a pupil of Messiaen thirty years before me. There is the greatest friendship between us now, but at that time it was not easy. He was a Schoenbergian – his father Walter Goehr had studied with Schoenberg – and had had a difficult relationship with Messiaen. In fact, he pushed me to broach subjects that Messiaen had never mentioned. In these weekly lessons above all we talked, and the extraordinary depth of his thinking bowled me over. What is the relation between the beginning and the end of a piece? Is everything rooted in the first bar? What is the nature of counterpoint? Is the sonority, the physical nature of music, of any importance? What is the relation between quantity and quality in music? The post-serial composers at this time thought that *quantity* (duration, dynamic, density . . .) was very important, but their conception of the *quality* of substance was often very primitive. We discussed a great deal. I was respectful, but it was sometimes quite tense. However, it made me reflect a lot and I think it liberated me from Messiaen's influence.

I remember the Duo for cello and piano that I wrote at Cambridge: a very violent piece, hard and expressionist. When I played it to Messiaen – I was still in contact with him and we corresponded regularly – he looked sad. He asked me, 'Has Professor Goehr made you listen to a lot of serial music?' At Cambridge, I also went to Robin Holloway, very different from Goehr. You could call him a neo-romantic, but that would be to over-simplify. We didn't always agree, but he is rich in ideas and his imagination is generous and sensitive.

The tuition that I received from Messiaen and Goehr was very different, with contradictory outlooks. I can't count the number of things that I learned from Messiaen, but equally it was Goehr who helped me to open the doors I wanted, even though I did not have the means to do so at that time. Over the years, I have also been lucky enough to get to know renowned composers like Henri Dutilleux and Elliott Carter. Equally, since my time at IRCAM, I very much value my contact with the extraordinary refinement and intellectual depth of Pierre Boulez.

In the end, confusion is profitable for a young composer; one comes under enormous influences that provoke many questions. Composition, as Ravel said, is choice, the choice of a single note, but also the choice of an aesthetic, and a philosophy.

While I was studying at Cambridge there were two important encounters. First of all, Oliver Knussen, who is eight years older than me. He is a great musician, a superb conductor and a marvellous composer. We spent entire days at his home, arguing into the early hours of the morning. He may be the composer with whom I have had the closest friendship. He made me aware of Elliott Carter and his extraordinary structural conceptions. He tried to convince me of the beauty of Schoenberg. We are also both conductors, and we both love to listen to all kinds of things, and have an enthusiastic curiosity about the history of music.

There was also Tristan Murail. One day I went to Messiaen's house, some time after my studies, and he mentioned that he had heard something wonderful. It was *Gondwana* by Murail. I asked for a tape, and I think I also wrote a letter to Tristan saying, 'Dear Sir, I have been told that your music is wonderful. Can we meet?'

Tristan's imagination is idiosyncratic and highly original. Since I met him in London, I think in 1981, we have been very good friends. Our first conversations were enthralling: his harmonic investigations, micro-intervals, sonic transformations, the pure timbre of his music. His music is a sort of dream in sound, a kind of multicoloured musical lava. We talked endlessly, mostly about aesthetics. He is passionate about processes and I am against; I don't like the obvious or didactic.

For me, musical invention has to have a kind of fantastical spontaneity on the surface, even if the underlying structure is strict. I don't like straight lines in music or art, except when they participate in an extremely lively dialectic between the rigid and the flexible. At this time, Tristan began to explore the computer and develop the most innovatory aspects of his music. His conception of harmony is genuinely original, and yet I have always thought that it is impossible to suppress melody in music completely. We have always argued about that. For him, melody was not really important and, where it does exist, it is a sort of secondary effect of harmonic processes. For me, melodic invention is essential. It was at that time that I became aware of one of the great problems in twentieth-century music: how to integrate the linear and vertical aspects. They are not different things, they are the same thing. If the emphasis is too much on one side, the results might be magnificent, but they will always be problematic.

MUSIC IN QUESTION

Thinking about harmony today

While I was at the Paris Conservatoire, I tried to find an original and authentic way of looking for chords. Now that seems to me both eccentric and yet useful. Music is a physical thing; it is sound, and that passes through the ears. It is not possible for a young composer to begin with a polyphonic and multidimensional style. You have to start with very simple things. Chords and composing harmonically are a good way to begin with music. Even in the oldest and most academic teaching methods you always start with harmony, with chorales, from the simplest to the most complex.

You first of all have to understand the physical aspect of musical sound, registers too, and how intervals change with the register. In the deepest bass, you can't hear anything, in the highest registers everything becomes pale, each interval changes in each register, each combination of intervals changes. That's the physical side, the sensual, almost primitive side. Then there is also the importance of musical knowledge, knowledge of tradition, even in a chord. If you produce a dominant seventh, ninth, thirteenth, you think of Debussy or Scriabin. If you study a certain chord from Berg's *Wozzeck,* you hear Wagner behind it. In each chord there are associations, memories that one can reject or exploit.

And there are aspects that are slightly more objective, even in a chord, for example the degree of diatonicism. If you produce a very dissonant chord where all the notes are diatonic the result is less harsh than a non-diatonic chord in which there are fewer notes. One must examine the numerous individual intervallic relationships, particularly between the bass and the highest note. There is also the fascinating area of resonance. After the individual chord there is the progression, the chord that comes next. Are there diatonic intervals between the parts? If the bass shifts by a fifth, a sort of cadence will result, even in an atonal context. Are there major triads implied within the progression? Does the progression constitute a mode? This is a simple way to enter into the universe of sound, to organize it and refine the ear. A good ear hears everything, each register, echoes of other styles, all harmonic implications. But it is essential also to feel. With Messiaen, when he played his own chords or some bars from *Pelléas* at the piano, one felt a profound emotion, a love for each note. One particular note in a specific context could be more important than two hundred thousand notes elsewhere because of a particular choice, be it tender or powerful.

But of course, that is not enough; one must study harmonic sensitivity and logic across the whole length of a structure – and it was only when I put aside my books of chords at the end of my studies with Messiaen, and what was in them became more intuitive, that I could begin to compose again. I needed something more flowing, more organic. And you can't achieve that with these vertical objects, it's impossible. To produce a structure that creates tension and can transform, you have to work with something more flexible.

Tradition

The question of harmony is perhaps the most important of this century. There is a big problem here – though problems are interesting, sometimes more than things that function successfully – which comes out of dodecaphonic thinking. If you use a series in an orthodox fashion, like Schoenberg and some of his successors, the problem is that the twelve notes move so quickly across a texture that there is no form of audible harmony. That means that the music has become almost entirely horizontal, the vertical aspect often being without any kind of control. The lines may perhaps be interesting but the vertical rules are only negative, 'against'; there are no rules 'for'. Besides, if the ear is constantly saturated with twelve notes repeating quickly across all registers it perceives only a harmonic chaos of limited interest. Chaos is only interesting if it is intended. This means there is no harmonic background, and thus there is no harmonic *rhythm*. Everything moves at the same speed. Without a hierarchy of speed within the motion of the notes, without perspective, there is no understanding of speed in music. Speed in music is not a question of rapid gestures, of the number of incidents. A monkey at a piano can hit the keys three hundred times a minute, but you would be wrong to think that it is making music equal in speed to the end of Beethoven's Seventh or *The Rite of Spring*. The speed and energy of the performer is not the same as that of the music. The energy of music is conceptual. And I'm convinced that there is a link between enharmony and the perception of movement. (By 'enharmony' I mean the change in function of unchanging pitches within mobile harmony, as when, in tonal harmony, the same held note takes on a different function by being 'spelt' differently, e.g., B♭/A♯ in two adjacent chords.) The problem with serial music is first and foremost the lack of poetry, of meaning, of harmonic control. But there is also a loss of speed and energy, everything that comes from mastery of harmony. These are terrible losses.

Certain composers have tried to hold on to the post-serial rules (no octaves, no tonality . . .) and to replace harmonic chaos with harmonic stasis. This kind of stasis is fashionable today. But the chords used are very complex acoustically and they are always novel. So they have to evolve slowly. Then all linear invention in this conception becomes a sort of arpeggiation of a fixed harmonic background. (The source of this technique is the wonderful first movement of Webern's symphony, opus 21.)

But if you want spontaneous, complex melodic phrases full of vitality, how do you assimilate them into such a rigid set-up? On the other hand, if you have lively and extremely varied melodies in a very rich counterpoint, how do you control the harmony? Another solution has been often employed since Ives: one mixes simultaneous polyphonies of melodies or harmonies along parallel streams, and the compositional conception relies entirely on superimposition. The results can be extraordinary, but often they are musically and structurally sterile. I think it is more interesting to have a more supple control over this problem.

The bass

There is another problem in the idea of harmony in today's music: the bass. It is simple: you play a long, loud single note in the bass, with very few other notes around it. A classical bass results. Everything that happens above relates to this bass note in a way reminiscent of tonal thinking. In some cases, if one wants less tension in the music, such a bass can be wonderful. I tried to use it in *At First Light*, especially in the third movement, in which a succession of bass notes creates functional implications.

Unfortunately, this kind of bass makes for an extremely rigid hierarchy in the texture. Everything above looks down and says, 'You are my master, I follow you.' That severely limits the freedom of behaviour above, harmonically and melodically. Nowadays, I'm interested in developing multi-dimensional forms. If the essence of the harmony and texture is in the bass, the invention above can't evolve in complete freedom. However, if you avoid the bass you cut out the register which gives warmth to sound. And, since music makes a physical impact, sonorous more than visual, without the bass the body doesn't respond in sympathy while listening. At the same time this kind of bass line implies a gigantic homophony and a conventional sense of harmonic perspective.

To get away from the quasi-functionality of the bass line, you have to curtail the resonance by using more than one note. I love the interval of a tenth, but that's even worse – it confirms the implications of the fundamental.

At First Light (extract). © 1982 Faber Music Ltd.
Reproduced by kind permission.

Tritones, ninths, sevenths, the type of interval in which the frequency ratios are not so simple, help produce a harmonic texture where the higher registers are freer and the bass line does not resonate in a functional manner. I have used this technique in the last of my *Three Inventions*. Often there are two notes, creating a sonorous but blurred bass, which avoid the resonance of a single pitch.

Moreover, if you don't have octaves, according to serial rules, and want to write a dark passage in the bass, you pick three notes below the viola's C and you get a sonic confusion which the ear finds extremely difficult to discern. If you want this confusion, a kind of acoustic chaos, that's fine – it's fantastic for thunder! (I exploited it throughout my first orchestral piece, *Ringed by the Flat Horizon*.) However, if you want a 'comprehensible' clarity, the use of a higher register (and octave doublings) will be needed.

Then there is the linear bass, which is not used much nowadays. This is a bass line where the notes sound only momentarily, giving a horizontal energy to the writing which doesn't give the bass time to settle, to resonate. This polyphonic bass, which doesn't function as a classical melodic bass, creates a kind of independent bass line (much used in my *Sudden Time*).

Three Inventions for Chamber Orchestra (no. 3: extract).
© 1995 Faber Music Ltd. Reproduced by kind permission.

Micro-intervals

I'm very fond of micro-intervals. They are easy to investigate with a computer, which is what I did for *Antara*. I invented virtual panpipes, where sampled and resynthesized panpipes are played back live via two keyboards (with extremely accurate micro-intervals) and combined with two solo flutes and orchestral strings. A semitone is actually a large interval, and when it is subdivided you can obtain very interesting melodic ideas. Also in *Antara* – and I don't know whether I succeeded in this – I wanted an intermediate field where the synthesized panpipes join the orchestral ensemble playing quarter tones, a kind of intermediate harmony.

It wasn't possible to have the panpipes in micro-intervals and the orchestra playing normal semitones: that would have sounded out of tune! There had to be a global harmonic conception. But it is difficult to play micro-intervals accurately on traditional instruments, even today. It can be achieved on strings, but not easily. I wanted it to be both playable and precise. The result is the style of the piece. The string and flute writing is often hocketed, as in the Middle Ages. This was also influenced by Andean panpipes which, because players need enormous effort to produce a single note (and disjunct legato is physically impossible), can only play in this manner. The melody is thus shared between two or more players. I thought that would be a good idea for the quarter tones, since it would give time to prepare fingerings. Thus the string writing is fragmented. This fragmentation interested me a great deal. If you create a musical object that appears to be unified but is in fact made up of fragments, you can perform extraordinary internal transformations.

This was one of my biggest lessons from the computer. It fascinated me that, without seeing how it's done, the computer could take a figurative image and seemlessly transform it into a completely different image, by cutting up the initial image into tiny fragments of colour, and transforming them in numerous abstract ways. It's like magic!

One can apply that to composition: beginning with an audible image, a thematic model, say, and by gradually changing many small fragments, transform it organically, without revealing the means. That has been a formal influence on me since *Relativity Rag* for piano and is still – much more than the manipulation of sound itself – the biggest remaining influence of the computer on my musical thought, since my long period of research at IRCAM. But that's another story.

The microtonal harmony in *Antara* was a sort of extension of my previous harmonic rules and knowledge, that I put to work in a new, more refined domain, with sometimes sixteenths of a tone inside chords, thanks to the computer. It is true that micro-intervals are stronger when the music is slow, when the ear has time to hear and assimilate the sounds. The stranger and more complex a sonority or harmony becomes, the longer the ear needs to hear it properly. That's why Gérard Grisey and Tristan Murail use such a broad harmonic rhythm, where the music goes from one chord to another very slowly. One has the time to perceive, understand and appreciate. But to avoid *Antara* being too static and the vertical aspect too dominant, I invented microtonal modes, to liberate the linear aspects of the piece. Often they are transposed or transformed while exploiting enharmonic interconnections, both short and long term. And at certain moments there is a sort of hyperchromaticism, where conjunct micro-intervals are restrained within a narrow tessitura. In this piece, the most important gamble – perhaps more than the fusion of natural and electronic sounds – was the attempt at integrating all these microtonal techniques.

There are lots of wonderful examples of the use of micro-intervals in non-western music. For instance, in Indian or Arab music, melodic thinking is extremely subtle and each slight intonation, each alteration is weighed against a background mode. Concentration is fixed on the adventure of a line in space. I am also interested in the tuning systems of Thailand and Bali, not to mention that of Burma (with its extraordinary timbres and, above all,

Antara (extract). © 1987 Faber Music Ltd. Reproduced by kind permission.

rhythms). Take, for example, the not-quite-whole-tone scale of Thailand, with seven notes to the octave rather than six, which our western ears interpret as a sort of out-of-tune diatonic scale. However, this interest in harmonic systems based on fixed scales can appear to be merely the craving for an exotic façade. In fact, Indian music seems to me more interesting with its inflections. Finally, of course, there remains the phenomenon of natural resonance, and it's true that nothing can match true, non-tempered intervals. They sound so beautiful. But we are composers, not just passive listeners; sound itself is not music.

Certainly, micro-intervals are fascinating, but if you want an active and dynamic music played by today's instruments, there are difficulties with accuracy. Also, if the music itself and the form are complex, there will be a perceptual overload. One won't hear them. To use new tuning methods honestly you have to create a simplified syntax and formal development. For now, I want to compose more active music and, to me, the constraint of twelve tones is very useful. If I wrote micro-intervallically, I would be forced to write simpler music.

There is also a curious link between structure and tuning. Without question, polyphony enables dynamic form. Form and polyphony are greatly reinforced by harmonic control and coherence. That is why the technique of polyphony integrated with harmony made such enormous progress with the arrival of equal temperament. One day I would love to write a piece that exploited another integrated temperament – like Huygens' system of thirty-one notes – but at the moment it could be played only by synthesizers.

Liberating form

Form has always been one of my absolute priorities. I have always felt the need to tackle organic concepts in music. Recently reading several books about chaos theory and having studied mathematics and chemistry at school, I have been fascinated by ideas of instability and, above all, the relation between simplicity and complexity. It seems that it was wrong to have separated chaos and order in the past; they are two manifestations of the same, unstable source. One is in the other. Many people are fascinated by fractals; they are very attractive, but less interesting. It is above all instability and the flexibility of morphology that it provokes, which has occupied me.

As I compose, I need the bars I am writing to link to the following ones, as if watching the process of something growing, but in a completely unexpected way. This kind of conception requires material that can grow and transform, but not in a simplistic or mechanical way. With too vertical a conception of music, one can't produce an interesting form. If the music is constantly controlled by vertical rules one can exploit any kind of internal decoration, but every time there is a vertical change there will be a gap. On the other hand, a really organic form is not constrained by breaks, it flows over them. Structure is the passage of material through time. Material in time can't always bump into partitions, or else the narrative of the music will be constantly broken. Polyphony permits a view of form that is really interesting because it allows a multidimensional concept of musical space. My greatest aim in *Sudden Time* was to liberate form by writing in a much more linear way than before, where all the audible harmony is nothing more than the result of the fusion of simultaneous lines. There is no trace of complex and static chords behind the texture. Many more interesting things could happen, therefore, I believe, in terms of syntax and dramatic growth, without mentioning the sense of motion and the virtuosity of the instrumental writing.

For sound as well. One could have a simultaneous heterogeneity: two, three, four, five, seven things happening at the same time, distinct yet comprehensible. If it is well written, the ear can hear numerous different things at the same time with great pleasure. Even at the time of Bach,

for instance, at the beginning of the *St John Passion*, there
are five contrasted layers.

In our time, unlike the classical or romantic periods,
composers have undoubtedly lost all conventional harmonic bearings. That may be unfortunate. Before, there
was an immediate and profound communication between
music and listener. On the other hand, in losing this 'con-
sensus' one has been liberated. One of the greatest achieve-
ments of the twentieth century, arising out of this loss, is
the liberation of form towards a sort of abstract narration.
When I speak of narration, I mean that material is
dynamic, capable of change, of transformation and combination with other material in other contexts. I take an
interval or two, a phrase, a very simple rhythmic element
and I start to mutate this simple material freely, without
constraints. In terms of rhythm, especially, one can do
much more interesting things than before.

On the harmonic level, in previous eras one specific chord
would be linked to each beat (in other words, the figured
bass). In the music I am writing now, there are pages where
potentially four or five simultaneous harmonic layers create
a kind of intentional confusion, superimposed in a complex
but controlled way. Suddenly, this can become a unified harmony. The beginning of Berg's *Altenberg Lieder* is an excel-
lent example of this: there are eight ostinato layers –
describing a snow storm – which gradually coalesce into a
single chord. The introduction to *Don Quixote* by Richard
Strauss is another example, basically more conventional, but
very audacious for its time. In a way, it is like a film director
who radically modifies the vantage point without cutting.

If all phenomena, the most heterogeneous and the most
homogeneous, issue from the same basic source, it is very
liberating. It requires huge organization. For the last five or
six years, if you looked at the sketches of my pieces you
would see an enormous amount of precomposition, which
would have horrified me when I was younger. I would
have found it without spontaneity, intuition, poetry. But
now, I make substructures – that themselves transform

Sudden Time (extract). © 1993 Faber Music Ltd.
Reproduced by kind permission.

across the whole structure – in order to arrive at an intuitive liberty, to liberate the form.

It is equally true that notation influences form.
Flexibility of notation is essential to open up the form. It is
like a painting, where the choice of brushes determines
how the painting will turn out. It is the same in music: the
tempo you choose, changing bar lengths, tempo relations,
techniques of sketching, all of this has a big influence.

What is the material?

Another valuable preoccupation in my recent music is that
the invention is *provoked* by timbre, though not *defined* by
it. This is a simple but important idea. When I compose, I
usually write straight into full score, I don't orchestrate.
This was the case with Sibelius and Janáček, two composers whom I admire greatly. I think of the sound as I
write the note. The thought of a specific instrument
inspires a specific kind of line. I am also fascinated by the
idea of orchestral space; it is something I think about constantly as I write. So the sound is essential, though, deep
down, the invention is independent of timbre. While I am
writing a certain type of material for four flutes or two cellos, say, I consider immediately how this material will
return in another, different instrumental guise, and not just
in order to vary the timbre. It is not only a question of sen-
suality, but of form. What stops form from becoming
organic is when the invention is imprisoned by timbre.

If I associate a particular material with the trumpet – as
I did in *At First Light* and especially in *A Mind of Winter* –
and if this constantly returns in the trumpet, what possibility is there for development? What can happen to it? The
listener responds, 'Ah, the trumpet's music!' This assists
recognition – it is interesting to perceive the same object in
ever-changing environments – and it is also useful for composing. But if I want to elaborate the material, I can't if I
have only two trumpets. A more serious problem: if I want

the material to become dark and menacing, I would have to place it in a low register. But I can't. If I want the material to be played very fast in an extremely high register, the idea collapses, since 'a trumpet can't do that'. On the other hand, if the material is not tied to one timbre, it can fly around, change speed, texture, timbre, in the imagination. Furthermore, any combination of materials is always conceivable, given the chosen instrumental forces. The structure can move from a homogenous mass (all the instruments playing the same kind of music) to extreme heterogeneity (where all the different kinds of material are heard simultaneously across the whole texture), with a lot of room for manoeuvring between both extremes.

If the identity of material is not in the timbre, it must be in the shape, the rhythm or in the intervals. Serialism actually taught me many things, notably in its notion of structure, where the potential for organic growth is very attractive. That can lead to an extreme diversity of material within a structure that remains coherent; a fascinating model. But superimposing heterogeneous material, in a post-modern way, is superficial. It exploits the surface of things instead of searching beneath and finding the deepest links within the diversity. A heterogeneity where everything can be combined, integrated and transformed in a profound way, with a real communication between materials, is much more interesting.

Being a composer

I go to lots of concerts and I often conduct other people's music. If I am struck by a piece, I wonder how it was written; I look at the score, I try to understand and to see if I can 'borrow' something. Very often, too, when my reaction is negative, that provokes me to search for the opposite. It is so difficult for me to start a piece. My imagination is fascinated by details, and not just simple ornamentation. In fact, the smallest element is essential as, in a dynamic structure, the tiniest detail can become the predominant foreground material.

At the beginning of a piece, if I have one useful hour a week, that's lucky! I am completely lost. The start of a new piece is at once a critique of the last piece and an exploration of new terrain. You have to do something different, find a new way of reinventing yourself. That happens when I look for something that hasn't worked in the previous piece.

I don't necessarily start my pieces at bar one. In *At First Light,* I began with the third movement. All the rhythmic and harmonic sketches that I made when I was with Messiaen were a kind of precomposition, exploring a territory that, at a certain moment, reached a certain maturity in my imagination, so that I could write a piece. Since then I have always worked in the same way. Before *Sudden Time,* I spent years investigating the perception of pulse, the tiny changes in duration that destroy a pulse, combinations of pulses, the idea of divisive rhythm within the pulse. I also explored an important field – one often ignored nowadays – which is an extension of divisive rhythm: metre, that is, the hierarchy of strong beats and accentuation. That can have deep implications for all sorts of areas such as the background figuration, melodic contour, harmonic rhythm, even structural intersection (that is, in a polyphonic texture, at what point do the individual lines change function or material). I wrote hundreds of pages, solely for the purposes of research, without thinking about a piece. At that point I also started to take pitch cells, much simpler than before, of three or five notes. I explored a kind of intervallic *Gestalt* to re-evaluate my concept of consonance and to avoid the mannerisms of post-serial melodic writing (full of ascending major sevenths).

The study of enharmony has been very important in this respect. I explored the capacity for mutation and combination of these tiny pitch cells, as if in a laboratory. Then at a certain point, inspiration strikes. What was cerebral in the laboratory suddenly becomes an expressive possibility and launches a piece. Nowadays, my procedure is less free than before. But

Three Inventions for Chamber Orchestra (no. 2: extract).
© 1995 Faber Music Ltd. Reproduced by kind permission.

even now I refuse to define a form before I start a piece. How is it possible to define what will happen to material before you get to know the material itself? For me, the material that I invent constructs its destiny, right in front of my eyes, as if I were at a play in which people meet and argue. If you invent material solely by intuition, starting at bar one without reflection, you're likely to get into exactly the kinds of formal difficulties that I would like to avoid. Things will follow by superimposition or by juxtaposition. Because there are no really deep points of contact, the formal continuity will be mono-dimensional and weak.

To avoid that, I invent a kind of terrain which gives the possibilities for connection and transformation within the materials: a flexible network of linked constraints. After working on this terrain I launch into the music itself and realize the possibilities of this material. It is like a playwright inventing characters, their manner, environment, their relationships, without knowing what the outcome is going to be. When I compose, I like to be surprised on the way; unforeseen things happen but nevertheless it must remain coherent. That is possible, if the initial conditions are well defined.

I need – but dislike – deadlines for my pieces. For the third of the *Three Inventions*, it took me nine months to write the first six or seven pages, and a month before the première by the Ensemble Modern in Salzburg the piece was still only half finished. It often happens that I go wrong; I make a false move, a bad decision – it's like taking a plant and cutting through the roots! Four weeks before the première, the half-composed piece died in front of me. The sketches became worse and worse, unbelievably bad. Eventually, I couldn't even write a note. So I went backwards and destroyed a quarter of what I'd written. Then I completed the rest in three weeks, at utmost speed. It is always like that. It takes me nine months to write the first half of a piece, and three weeks to finish it. In a frenzy! I don't sleep; it's a kind of madness. It is invigorating, but I couldn't live the whole of my life with such intensity.

Teaching

I teach composition at the Royal College of Music in London. What interests me is to learn. I have to study, analyze, reflect and arrange my thoughts appropriately and clearly in order to explain them. Occasionally in class I touch on my personal preoccupations before beginning a piece, things that trouble or fascinate me. If I think of what I have done in the past few years, I take an abstract idea and choose numerous different examples to stimulate reflection in my students. For instance; take the history of dynamics in music. It is so simple: from *piano* to *forte*, almost nothing. But you can trace with this the evolution of formal concepts across the history of music!

Another subject: how to start a piece. Looking at the first bars of Beethoven's nine symphonies is always a surprise, unexpected. The First Symphony begins in the wrong key, the Fourth with extraordinary mysterious octaves. And as for the Ninth, it has an almost Darwinian beginning.

One can study the history of pulse. I devoted two courses of six hours to it. Questions of rubato, duration, pulse, metre . . .

And then more specific subjects: polyrhythms in Stravinsky, the last act of *Wozzeck*, Boulez's fourth orchestral *Notation*, Carter's Concerto for Orchestra, *Le gibet* by Ravel, Beethoven's last piano sonata, a detailed investigation of the famous six-voice *Ricercare* by Bach, and various analyses of modern works.

Sometimes I invite a guest to speak. A viol player came to demonstrate that wonderful instrument. Great Indian musicians have come, an expert in Russian music, all sorts of interesting people to expand our thinking. I have done this about once a month; the students come to my home on Sunday at about 11 o'clock and leave around 6, though sometimes they stay until midnight. When I gave a course about *Sudden Time* there were twenty-nine of them in my living room! I don't know whether it is useful for them, though it gives me a lot. It pleases me very much to have both British and foreign students. It has also been a privilege for me to have been invited to speak far afield; I remember particularly visiting Peking and Shanghai Conservatories in 1993, where the warmth of the people and their generosity of spirit were very touching.

Pointers

When I was young I didn't like Bach at all, but I have changed. Listen to his fugues: each voice traces a beautiful and expressive line and, at the same time, all together they make luminous harmonies. What's interesting with him is the fusion of harmony and melody. The vertical is already present in his polyphonic themes. Each line integrates conjunct scalic passages with disjunct chordal arpeggiation, involving a constant, supple interchange between both. I think that he achieves the most profound assimilation between the vertical and the horizontal in any western music.

I don't really like Hindemith. I regard Bartók as a great composer, very original, but there are certain traits that I don't like very much. For instance, the kind of diatonic harmony with 'false notes', major chords in the left hand with a melody in another mode which gives a sort of facile polytonality. There's his manner of imitation, often by inversion, with phrases that are rhythmically rather square. Then there is a certain coldness of sound and expression that isn't really to my taste. But pieces like *The Miraculous Mandarin* and the *Music for Strings, Percussion and Celesta* are wonderful. If I had to choose an eastern European composer from the early years of this century, perhaps I would choose Janáček. Janáček had such a generous heart; I'm thinking particularly of *Kat'a Kabanová* or *The Cunning Little Vixen*. Even though his technique was rather primitive, it was also highly inventive. He is one of the few composers of the twentieth century to have invented an authentic melodic style that is both extremely personal and very expressive.

As to the question of Adorno's choice between Stravinsky and Schoenberg, I would first answer that I wouldn't choose Adorno. On a good day he is wonderful. He was responsible for perhaps the best writing on music that I have ever encountered. But in some contexts he is so dogmatic. His post-war pessimism was maybe understand-able, but so severe, even cruel, that I could never accept it. One has the impression of an intellectual tyranny. In his studies on Berg, when he analyzes the actual music, he is rather conventional. Then, all of a sudden, he thinks of Stravinsky and proposes absurd arguments against him. On the other hand, when he speaks in more general terms about Berg or Mahler, in a non-analytical vocabulary, it is wonderful. His essay about Berg in *Quasi una fantasia* illustrates the spirit of his teacher with an extraordinary sensitivity and empathy.

To return to Schoenberg and Stravinsky, they are both great composers. Schoenberg's philosophical ideas interest me more than Stravinsky's. But for the sheer sound I would choose Stravinsky every time. I prefer the personal-ity of his music. The *Symphony of Psalms*, *Les Noces*, the *Symphonies of Wind Instruments*, *Movements* for piano and orchestra, *Ebony Concerto*, *The Rite of Spring*, *Petrushka*; this is music of dazzling brilliance.

Debussy is a giant. Imagine his meeting with Stravinsky in Paris ninety years ago! With Debussy, there is a flexibil-ity, a freedom of writing, an intimate sensitivity that is quite unique. I have always thought that Debussy's inventiveness was extraordinary, for instance in the last *Etudes*. I have also always adored Ravel. He has more clarity, there is less ambiguity and mystery than with Debussy, but technically, my word! *La Valse* or *Daphnis et Chloé* display such con-summate craftsmanship and compositional virtuosity. Ravel's music is provocative. He exposes problems and sug-gests solutions, yet always with such expressive subtlety. I have performed several of his pieces myself as a pianist, among them *Valses nobles et sentimentales* and the wonderful *Ma Mère l'Oye*.

These days I prefer conducting to playing the piano. I usually give no more than ten concerts a year – I am aware of the dangers for a composer of going down that route – but my repertoire is quite varied. As well as my own works, I've often conducted works by the great contemporary figures like Messiaen, Ligeti, Boulez or Berio. At the same time, I conduct many works by composers nearer my own age (Tristan Murail, Gérard Grisey, Unsuk Chin, Wolfgang Rihm, Denys Bouliane) as well as several earlier twentieth-century masters (Stravinsky, Ravel, Sibelius, Varèse, Berg), and even a few from the nineteenth century. Amongst British composers, I have sometimes conducted beautiful works by Harrison Birtwistle, Oliver Knussen, Jonathan Harvey and Simon Holt.

Towards opera

My own musical roots are in the theatre, with my experiences of theatre music at school and university, not to mention the large number of silent films that I have accompanied, improvising at the piano. Maybe I am not made for collaborating, but I would certainly like to write an opera. In contemporary opera, the big problem is the vocal writing. Opera is song, and song is melody. I don't mean melody like Verdi or *Carmen*, but some improvement is essential, for the future of opera. Since serialism, melodic intervals have tended towards a sort of mannerism, a caricature of modern music, exploiting disjunct, zigzag shapes. That's not easy to change, but I took up the challenge in my piece *Upon Silence*.

Another thing that is difficult in opera – with characters who cross the stage, the orchestra, the degree of activity – is that, if the harmonic style is too complex, the listener–spectator finds it difficult to assimilate the voice with the orchestra. The twentieth century has made wonderfully

Upon Silence (extract). © 1991 Faber Music Ltd.
Reproduced by kind permission.

rich discoveries in form, rhythm, timbre, but, compared with other centuries, it is weaker in the area of melody. Narrative has also become problematic, for the simple reason that the nineteenth century so magnified it. Besides, it is the cinema which satisfies our cultural needs for great narrative myths nowadays. Perhaps one of the future avenues for opera, which took so much from the nineteenth-century novel, will be to derive inspiration from the cinema.

Music and theatre existed together even before instruments and notation. I am sure that it was one of the origins of music. It ought to be possible to reinvent it. Perhaps one has to have a certain naivety to write operas; you have to believe in the medium. We are no longer in the period of Verdi or Wagner, where you were constantly surrounded with magnificent operas. Still, despite everything, there is a lot more energy in opera now than twenty years ago, so nothing is impossible!

Survey

(1978–96)

Renaud Machart

Given his exceptional pianistic gifts, it comes as no surprise to find that George Benjamin's first major work was a Piano Sonata, completed in 1978 when he had just turned eighteen. Composed whilst he was a pupil of Olivier Messiaen at the Paris Conservatoire, the Sonata is in the somewhat Lisztian form of a single continuous movement divided into three contrasted sections. The piece is extremely virtuosic, packed almost to the point of bursting with ideas and textures: indeed, its explosive concentration of contrasting musical characters has certain parallels with other single movement sonata forms from earlier in the century, such as Schoenberg's First Chamber Symphony, op. 9 (1906). The piece certainly reveals a good deal about Benjamin's tastes and training: Debussy, Ravel and Messiaen are all in evidence – the second movement's obsessively re-iterated single pitches recall Ravel's *Le Gibet*, whilst its harmonic language is rather reminiscent of Messiaen. In retrospect, however, we find little in the Sonata of Benjamin's later compositional language.

Between 1981 and 1985 Benjamin composed four more piano pieces. He readily acknowledges that he no longer cares much for *Sortilèges* (1982), the piece in which the influence of Messiaen can perhaps be most clearly heard. He is much more fond of The Three Piano Studies (1984–6) on the other hand, 'thanks to the extraordinary pianist Pierre-Laurent Aimard, who plays them like no-one else.' While the Sonata suffers if anything from an excess of compositional freedom, the tight, self-imposed discipline of each of the Three Studies provides a perfect control for both expressive and formal needs.

The Piano Sonata was followed by the Octet (1979),

composed when Benjamin had begun his period of study at
Cambridge. The piece is scored for a standard mixture of
solo wind and strings – though without oboe or trumpet,
instruments that would be central to Benjamin's later
chamber pieces – plus a single percussionist and an important, almost soloistic part for celesta. The Octet has a pre-
dominantly hectic character, with wide intervallic leaps,
irregular rhythmic patterns and frequent changes of metre.
The only respite from all this activity is the 'Misterioso'
section (starting at bar 94), a slow and melancholy passage
looking forward to *Ringed by the Flat Horizon* and *At
First Light*, with glistening string harmonics, trills and liquid figurations on celesta and tuned percussion, and a
prominent piccolo solo. Beneath its modernist surface, the
piece is built on an almost classical plan of fast–slow–fast,
framed by an introduction and coda.

It was an orchestral piece begun in Paris, *Ringed by the
Flat Horizon* (1978–9), which first put Benjamin's name
on the international music scene, thanks to its performance
to five thousand people at the London Proms in 1980. Its
title comes from *The Waste Land* by T. S. Eliot:

> Who are these hooded hordes swarming
> Over endless plains, stumbling in cracked earth
> Ringed by the Flat Horizon only
> What is the city over the mountains
> Cracks and reforms and bursts in the violet air.

The other inspiration for the work was a dramatic photograph of a storm breaking over the New Mexico desert.
As with the pictorial inspiration of *At First Light*,
Benjamin is not content with the mere description of this
photograph in sound: rather, he uses the picture to prompt
analogies with his rich palette of orchestral colours, forming poetic correspondences between the two.
    Ringed by the Flat Horizon does not follow a pre-defined
programme: its musical progress is dictated by playing off
fluctuating and static elements against each other in con-

stantly changing combinations. Yet, despite the hybrid
nature of the work's form, it is handled with considerable
mastery.

A few highlights of the score: the cunningly altered return
of the opening bell-chords (at letter F in the score), now
accompanied by string harmonics; an intense, lyrical climax
featuring a taut cello solo (letter O); piercingly dense wind
chords, (letter X); and a first violin melody of Bergian
intensity (letter Z). The music winds down to a sequence
series of leaden, threatening chords, marked 'Solemn and
Dark' (letter GG). Solos emerge from this tense atmosphere
(trombone, high trumpet) before the storm finally breaks at
letter NN; the work ends with a return to the wind solos of
the opening passage – cor anglais, oboe and flutes, this time
adding the solo cello (distantly recalling the middle section),
until all dissolves into the concluding, glacial bell-chord.

In deliberate contrast to the tone of unease and menace
in much of *Ringed by the Flat Horizon*, Benjamin's second
orchestral work is transparent, numinous. The title *A
Mind of Winter* (1980–1) comes from a poem of Wallace
Stevens, 'The Snowman'. Scored for soprano and Mozart-
sized orchestra, it seems at first simpler than *Ringed by the
Flat Horizon*, possibly due to the presence of a text. The
vocal line, which consists mostly of long sustained notes, is
very much instrumental in manner, a feature that recurs in
the vocal piece *Upon Silence*. But the difference between
Benjamin in 1980 and 1990 lies in his conception of
polyphony. In *A Mind of Winter* the voice emerges imper-
ceptibly out of the general orchestral sonority, but forms
no part of the orchestra's complex polyphony. It is surrounded by a dense halo of string textures, with a strong
flavour of A minor – but this A minor is constantly
clouded and obscured by delicate webs of chromatic filigree, which blur the harmonic focus. The textures readily
evoke certain images from the text: gusts of wind in glissandi and harmonics on muted strings; snow in the transparent, crystalline figurations on piccolos and the pervasive
hiss of sizzle cymbals ('Of the pine trees crusted with

A Mind of Winter (extract). © 1981 Faber Music Ltd.
Reproduced by kind permission.

snow', letter F *et seq*.). The writing is subtle and evanescent, never gratuitous, and always designed to produce an
audible effect. Benjamin allocates solos to what became his
favoured instruments: oboe and muted piccolo trumpet
(both of them play obbligato roles in *At First Light*).

The end of *A Mind of Winter* seems to evoke a variety
of earlier works: Schoenberg's Second String Quartet, pos-

sibly, or Darius Milhaud's little-known but extraordinary Second Quartet – both of which feature important obbligato parts for voice; perhaps even the *Four Last Songs* of Richard Strauss. The voice conveys the desolate, enigmatic image of the concluding line, evoking the 'Nothing that is not there and the nothing that is', as the music drifts to a hushed close. *A Mind of Winter* draws the listener into an ambiguous, uncertain, dream-like world, the realm of the 'intermezzo' (in Roland Barthes' phrase describing Schumann*), the realm of twilight, of the 'distant glimmer of the January sun', to quote Wallace Steven's poem.

Taking a new tack, George Benjamin conceived his third large-scale work for the standard line-up of twentieth century ensemble: the forces of the London Sinfonietta, who commissioned the piece. *At First Light* (1982) again refers to an image, this time a painting by Turner called 'Norham Castle, Sunrise', now in the Tate Gallery. This canvas, reproduced on the cover of the score, is one of the painter's most famous, and its subtlety and depth of colour, its 'liquefaction' of forms, was to have a huge influence on impressionist techniques. The enigmatic content of the painting is not so much a composition as a 'decomposition', with the few identifiable figures seemingly dissolving in the sunlight: it isn't hard to imagine what sort of a sound world this might give rise to. But how can a composer suggest solid and liquid shapes in sound, contrast them or transform them into each other?

To some extent *At First Light* makes an interesting synthesis between the active complexity of *Ringed by the Flat Horizon* and the contemplative blankness of *A Mind of Winter*. Those two pieces had plainly demonstrated Benjamin's talents as an orchestrator. After *A Mind of Winter* there was a possible danger that Benjamin's music would become too sensual, too dazzling, that it would become merely 'atmospheric'. *At First Light* showed quite

---

*See Roland Barthes' 'Loving Schumann' in *The Responsibility of Forms*, Oxford: Basil Blackwell, 1986, pp. 295–6.

the reverse, that those qualities of colour could be put at the service of a form and discourse which, although frequently poetic, is nonetheless rigorous and strong.

The beginning of the first of three main sections in *At First Light* is an enigmatic introduction with a texture that could almost have come from *A Mind of Winter* – string harmonics, fleeting woodwind figures, bowed vibraphone, solo piccolo trumpet . It lasts just a few bars, before a flurry of grace notes, several resonant chords and a final shimmering trill lead into the second movement, which is in fact the first main part of the work proper.

By stark contrast, the elements are now concrete, low and harsh, with scrapings on the double bass, clusters on low piano and repeated, sharp punctuations on suspended cymbal – a stark, rude texture. After a while, the music is becalmed in a slow section featuring a minor third drone in the clarinet and horn (letter H in the score). The celesta and vibraphone answer with spidery, transparent figures against a background of held string harmonies. At letter K the rasping, rude elements return, this time featuring a solo viola with crushed bowing. Bell chords on the piano (used as a percussion instrument) and flurries of grace notes (*à la* Pierre Boulez) are worked up to a point of exasperation before freezing on an unstable augmented fourth, initiated by the piccolo trumpet and now taken up by the whole ensemble (letter T).

What follows could be regarded as a transition, in which all the elements seem to dissolve, as figures in the painting appear decayed: string harmonics, breath noises on wind and brass, a ping-pong ball bounced in a glass, the sounds of torn paper (these last two used for the nature of their sound rather than as theatrical gimmicks), taps on the piano lid, and so on. The music has reached a point of total dissolution.

Quite suddenly, these scattered, evanescent sounds coalesce into a resonant harmonic sequence for the entire ensemble (minus the piano and percussion). This is the opening of the third movement, surely one of the most

beautiful passages in Benjamin's music, the rich harmony
oscillating gently between pairs of chords. Soon volatile
instrumental figurations burst out of this stable material,
and the music veers alternately between becalmed passages
for a few instruments and renewed surges of energy for the
whole ensemble. A series of particularly sonorous chords
(Benjamin marks them 'majestic' several times) leads
towards a climax of incredible, almost orchestral force (letter J): over a low C (trombone, double bass and contrabassoon in octaves), a radiant chord of natural harmonics
blossoms into a texture somewhat reminiscent in its harmonic style of the 'spectral' composers Tristan Murail and
Gerard Grisey, whose work Benjamin was discovering
around this time. This highpoint of energy explodes and
dies away in a tam-tam resonance. A short coda to the
whole work bolts off unexpectedly in a shrill concluding
flourish not unlike the end of Stravinsky's *Rite of Spring*.

In common with many British composers, George
Benjamin has received commissions whose prime aim is
educational. In Benjamin's case the result was *Jubilation*
(1985), a piece for large orchestral group, including, apart
from the usual players, a children's chorus, a synthesizer,
extra groups of recorders, brass, steel drums and untuned
percussion played by children. Though the piece has a
basically clear D major tonic, this is not Benjamin 'tidied
up' for the children: the material given to the recorders is
not simple, especially when one remembers that each line
is played by up to ten performers at the unison.

Given its prevalently celebratory atmosphere, *Jubilation*
is well named. Yet the D–F♯ major third, introduced by the
synthesizer, is soon twisted and distorted, and the music's
stability is disintegrated by the synthesizer into a rich, complex chord (again recalling the 'spectral' composers). The
children's choir sings *solfège* very clearly in D major,
although there is only one sharp in the key signature, C♯
being absent from this section. The arrival of C♮, forming a
tritone (C♮–F♯) doubled on piccolo trumpet, recalls an

At First Light (extract). © 1982 Faber Music Ltd.
Reproduced by kind permission.

equivalent point at the end of the first movement of *At First Light* (letter D). A group of steel drums lends the music a Balinese colour which Benjamin is fond of and which recurs, in different ways, in *Antara*, *Sudden Time* and the *Three Inventions*. The two groups of recorders (between one and ten players – Benjamin indicates the numbers very precisely) enter playing running and scalic figures. As in *Antara*, two types of flute – here recorders and normal flutes – play antiphonally in dialogue with each other (in *Antara* the same happens between synthe-sized panpipes and flutes). Because of its unusual instru-mentation *Jubilation* is not played very often which is a shame: it has a central place in Benjamin's output, both on technical and emotional grounds: a rare example of a piece in which exuberance is not tempered with melancholy.

At the Paris première by the London Sinfonietta of *At First Light* in 1983, Pierre Boulez was impressed by Benjamin's music and during the summers of 1984 and 1985 Benjamin was invited to study electronics and digital techniques, particularly those of the 4X computer, devel-oped towards the end of the seventies by Guiseppe di Giugno. However, it wasn't the ultra-sophisticated 4X that attracted the composer, but meeting a group of South American panpipe players busking outside the Pompidou Centre (see pp. 77–8). It is tempting to think of the young composer, lost in IRCAM's cave of modern technology, finding solace in the straightforward music-making taking place outside the building. In reality, Benjamin was simply struck by the sonority of the pan-pipes, recreated this sonor-ity and developed it in numerous ways with the help of the technology. Intuitively, he used the latter as a tool and means of expression, not as an end in itself. A short prepara-tory study for tape laid the foundations: *Panorama* (1985) manipulates the panpipe sound and sets it in motion through space, in a manner not dissimilar from *Antara* itself.

The first version of *Antara* is scored for instrumental ensemble (two flutes, two trombones, percussion, three violins, two violas, two cellos and double bass) and 4X computer. But this encountered the same difficulties that have hindered Pierre Boulez's *Répons*, namely that the size of the 4X reduces the possibilities of performance outside IRCAM. A version was prepared with a tape containing the 4X's part, synchronized by the conductor hearing a click track through headphones. Still, the real virtue of *Antara* lies in its use of live electronics to permit flexibility in time, with all the pan-pipe sounds triggered by two live performers at synthesizer keyboards: this ensures that technology is subordinate to the tempo of the conductor, not the other way round.*

The two synthesizers basically produce panpipe sounds, from extremely rapid passagework to very rich chords; they also provide percussive effects (derived from striking the metal girders of the Pompidou Centre itself!) and breath sounds (amplified samples of the sound from the embouchure of panpipes, chopped up and treated). The score makes great use of micro-intervals, both in the instrumental and the electronic parts. On the harmonic front, this enables Benjamin to explore the particular sound-qualities of chords derived from just intonation; melodically, the 4X makes possible what otherwise would be unplayable, notably extra-fast panpipe figures with any imaginable microtonal refinement.

The most notable thing about *Antara* is probably the way the composer deploys the idea of two antiphonal choirs of flute sonority, real flutes and electronic panpipes. The resultant antiphonal play between the two sonorities, as they echo and respond to each other in ever-changing hockets, exploits the similarities and differences of the two sound worlds to the full. *Antara* initiated a new phase in Benjamin's conception of polyphony, a more linear and abstract style, with less reliance on purely coloristic phenomena. Nevertheless there are many passages of great poetry: the haunting use of breath sounds from letter S onwards, and

---

*In 1992, the 4X part of *Antara* was transferred to the IRCAM workstation, which runs on the NEXT computer.

Antara (extract). © 1987 Faber Music Ltd. Reproduced by kind permission.

particularly in the *Misterioso* sections of the central slow movement. There is a good deal of compositional *joie-de-vivre*, too, especially throughout the faster passages of the work, notably the ebullient coda: gentle string skittering provides a featherlight background for a playful two-voice melody on piccolos. This passage is punctuated by several appearances of what Benjamin terms a 'hybrid' sound – a computer-generated fusion of the panpipe sonorities with the Pompidou Centre's metal girders: the result is a complex, evolving spectrum of great beauty, a breathy sonority blossoming into a gleaming metallic sheen.

Antara – the first large-scale composition from Benjamin's pen since *At First Light* (1982), we should remember – was the product of many years' conscientious reflection and compositional research. Following its completion, Benjamin again ran into difficulties with the nature and evolution of his own musical language. He had begun work on a large orchestral project back in 1983; he now resumed this project, and continued working on it sporadically from 1989 to 1993, interrupted by long periods of unease.

During this difficult period for the composer, the one oasis of inspiration and freshness was the surprising and decisive piece *Upon Silence*, in 1990. Two years earlier he had been the featured composer at the early music festival at Saintes, where his music was played along with that of Henry Purcell. Shortly afterwards, Benjamin came across Nikolaus Harnoncourt's recording of the Purcell viol fantasies and, as with panpipes five years before, he was struck by the freshness of viola da gamba sonorities, so different from those of the violin family. Benjamin was equally struck by the polyphonic elaboration of these sonatas written 'in the olden style', the most densely complex music Purcell ever composed. He immediately conceived the idea to compose a piece of his own for viol consort, collaborating to this end with the British viol group 'Fretwork'. In the event, he chose to add a part for solo voice – a mezzo soprano – and turned the new project into his second vocal work, *Upon Silence,* for mezzo and five viols, composed between 1989 and 1990.

At first hearing, *Upon Silence* curiously evokes a consort song or a Franco-Flemish *chanson* of the sixteenth century. At that time such polyphonic pieces (mostly for between three and seven voices) could be played in several different versions, for instruments or voices alone, or for the two together. If in his musical language Benjamin distances himself completely from any ancient model, he retains one crucial basic principle, the instrumental character of the vocal part, joining in the overall polyphony. The voice part alternates between long notes (like a *cantus firmus*) and a very virtuosic style, like the florid voice writing in English Renaissance polyphony.

The text is by W. B. Yeats (1865–1939), 'The Long-legged Fly'. The musical structure of the piece follows the tripartite form of the poem (see Benjamin's description, p. 76). A meditative narrative (in couplets) describing three different characters in succession alternates with a decorative vocalise on Yeats' refrain, which becomes longer on each occurrence:

> Like a long-legged fly upon the stream
> His (Her) mind moves upon silence.

The rather melancholic character of *Upon Silence* is partly due to the essentially plaintive tone-quality of the viols; but it is surely also due to the dedication of the piece to the memory of Michael Vyner – the artistic director of the London Sinfonietta and a loyal friend and supporter of Benjamin – who died in 1989. This suggests that the piece, over and above the tone of the poem, is really an elegy, very much in keeping with the desolate character of the Purcell fantasies, which initially inspired Benjamin. (In 1995, Benjamin was commissioned to transcribe one of Purcell's fantasies for the tercentenary of the composer's death. He chose the one in C minor, composed on 19 June 1680, and transposed it to G minor for a quartet of B♭ clarinet, violin, cello and celesta.)

For reasons of practicality Benjamin was obliged to transcribe *Upon Silence* for a standard string ensemble (in this form it was premièred in Paris in March 1992); viol consorts are rare, and rarer still are those who would dare to perform such a difficult piece, especially since it requires a conductor. In order to compensate for the loss of the exceptional richness of the viols' sonority, Benjamin added two extra instruments to the group: two violas, three cellos, two double basses, all muted. The polyphony is modified here and there, with a few added lines (compare, for example, the two versions at letter K). *Upon Silence* marks the advent of a new characteristic in Benjamin's writing, already glimpsed in *Antara*: the contrapuntal dimension. Eschewing the harmonic richness of earlier works, the music is conceived horizontally, with events superimposed running at different speeds simultaneously.

Sudden Time (1989–93) is probably Benjamin's most important work to date – a key work in its scope and ambition, as indicated by the time it took (ten years all told) and the terrible difficulties that had to be overcome to compose it.

A new style had already emerged in 1990 with *Upon Silence*, but it took the composer a further three years to complete the piece originally commissioned by the Südwestfunk for a performance in 1989. That commission was cancelled, leaving only an orchestral fragment lasting a few minutes, *Cascade*, which had actually been sketched between 1983 and 1989. It became the first few pages of *Sudden Time* (up to the pause at letter N in the score) with the addition of a short coda which was removed in the final version of the piece.

The first thing that one notices when hearing *Sudden Time* is that the sensual and evocative universe of the early pieces has given way to a more austere style. While some of his colleagues succumbed to the siren song of neo-tonality, and while the peculiar intimacy of *Upon Silence* might have hinted that Benjamin would go in a completely different direction, *Sudden Time* pursues the technical discoveries of the viol piece in quite a radical manner. It's a large, abstract canvas, which evolves in broadly spaced musical paragraphs of great energy, complex without seeming complicated (to paraphrase Ravel's famous dictum). The piece is in a state of constant renewal, where each new element is smoothly absorbed into the ongoing flux of the music. Benjamin says that the title – a quote from Wallace Stevens – should be understood as referring to these sudden, fleeting appearances of recognizable, predictable elements (regular pulsation or metrical patterns) within a universe of ceaseless transformation and change.

Perhaps more than in any other work of Benjamin, one is struck by the apparent ease with which he manages to manipulate long stretches of musical time and give the effect of great continuity of movement – a feature which recalls Sibelius's Seventh Symphony, a work which Benjamin holds in very high regard. Benjamin's orchestration in *Sudden Time* shows the same unerring exactitude of ear for colours and their balancing as any of his earlier pieces, but here these virtues are put at the service of a much more freely evolving and fluid musical syntax. Without going into detailed analysis, several features stand out as being of especial import in the flow of the music: the viola da gamba sonority obtained through string harmonics at letter N (just after the pause); a supple and sinuous cor anglais solo accompanied by harp, a combination faintly reminiscent of Mahler (letter W); a group of four alto flutes recalling the virtuoso figures of *Antara* (letter F); another of Benjamin's imaginary Balinese gamelans (four bars before letter H) rendered here by the unusual combination of resonant pizzicati on double basses, muted upright piano and high timpani. Finally the magnificent coda, with its extraordinarily high viola solo (four bars after Z), a part that could be played with greater suppleness, if assigned to a violin, but which would thereby lose its particular intensity and tension. In fact, in *Sudden Time* as a whole, Benjamin seems to forsake the brighter solo instruments (oboes, trumpets) that he favoured in earlier works in favour of lower, darker, more

Sudden Time (extract). © 1993 Faber Music Ltd.
Reproduced by kind permission.

vulnerable sonorities – alto flutes, cor anglais, viola.

The scoring of *Three Inventions for Chamber Orchestra* (1993–5) for twenty-four players is a return to the set-up of *At First Light*, but noticeably enlarged – an additional flute, two more clarinets, an extra horn, an additional percussionist, a harp, and a string section now comprising three violins with pairs of violas, cellos and basses. The sound world of the Inventions is very far from *At First Light* – the ordeal of composing *Sudden Time* had radically transformed Benjamin's style. Indeed, the Inventions seem to share a number of prominent features with *Sudden Time*: the continuously evolving form of each invention is clearly a product of the formal innovations in the orchestral piece, the polyphonic writing has a similar linear fluidity, and there are even one or two similar sonorities: the preference for the lower and less common instruments such as Flugel-horn (in the first invention), cor anglais (in the second), and a telling use of contrabassoon and euphonium in the last invention; and the combination of pizzicato strings, harp and piano in the first invention is clearly reminiscent of similar textures in *Sudden Time*.

The Three Inventions also take the exploration of pentatonic modes in *Sudden Time* several stages further. One of the most remarkable and unexpected features of Benjamin's recent music is indeed its unaffected re-discovery of the pentatonic mode, the 'primal mode of music' as Bartók termed it. If gamelan-like sonorities return at the opening of the first invention, then other exotic musics lie behind the following two movements: the incredibly swift, seemingly chaotic metres and strident timbres of Burmese court music inspired Invention 2; whilst the third's slowly drifting pentatonic chords in string harmonics were suggested by the high, cluster-like harmony of the *sho*, a Japanese mouth-organ.

The Three Inventions are sharply contrasted from each other. The First Invention begins with a gamelan of harp, vibraphone and pizzicato strings. The arrival of the Flugelhorn solo (on page 8) which henceforth dominates the texture, oddly recalls the elegiac sentiment of Aaron Copland's *Quiet City* (1939), where the trumpet and cor anglais play a leading role.

The cor anglais once again takes the solo role in the Second Invention. This is more overtly rhythmic, even violent; the texture is underpinned by pizzicato strings with the harp, all strumming vigorously like some huge guitar. As this hectic texture seems to be reaching a climax the frenzy is heightened by the arrival of a wild clarinet solo, in the upper extremes of the instrument's range; like its predecessor, this movement is cut off without warning.

The Third Invention, by far the longest of the three, is quite unlike anything else in Benjamin's output. Its most obvious feature is the almost claustrophobic predominance of extremely low sonorities which run through the entire movement in some form or other from start to finish. It opens with a strange, extended contrabassoon solo, accompanied by a bizarre assortment of sounds: slow, downward slides on muted trombone and low strings, with sudden punctuations on bass drum, tuned gongs (with their resonance cut off) and non-vibrato chords on viola, cello, and bass. Only the occasional luminous octaves from the harp and celesta lighten the heavy, doom-laden atmosphere. This Third Invention, harsh and feverish, builds to an impressively tumultuous polyrhythmic climax, with ever more ominous thuds from two bass drums bestriding the texture, before it too is cut off abruptly – by a final, deafening drum-stroke from both percussionists in unison. On the surface this is one of its composer's least outwardly seductive pieces. It is certainly a long way from the transparent colours of *At First Light*. But the razor-sharp ear with which it is put together, and the unremitting, almost suffocating intensity with which the music unfolds are quite breathtaking.

Compositions

Notes by George Benjamin

Sonata for Violin and Piano

25 mins
Composed: April 1976 to February 1977
First performance: London, Westminster School,
27 May 1977, Charles Peebles (violin), George
Benjamin (piano)
Score and part 0 571 51758 7 on sale

This three-movement work is above all a sonata
for violin *and* piano, not a sonata for violin with
piano accompaniment. It was written during my
final years at school in London.

The first and last movements, though often
changeable in mood, follow a 'slow–fast–slow'
structural pattern, in which reflective, slow duos
contrast with more dynamic interaction between
the instruments. The central scherzo, which exploits
a few unexpected sonorities, maintains its quick
tempo as it builds towards an explosive conclusion.

Altitude

9 minutes
Brass band
Composed: July to September 1977
Written for Elgar Howarth and the Grimethorpe
Colliery Brass Band
First performance: York University, 12 May
1979, Grimethorpe Colliery Brass Band, Elgar
Howarth (conductor)
Full score and parts for hire

Altitude was written in the summer of 1977, at

the request of Elgar Howarth. The music portrays
an imaginary flight at an extreme height – cold,
solitary, tranquil and yet swift and mobile.

The form is roughly as follows:

1 A fast, but harmonically static, opening section,
   with a long melody in the tubas
2 A slower more flowing section, beginning with a
   descending theme played by a solo cornet
3 Tense development of previous material, culminating in a full fortissimo statement of the cornet's theme
4 A long, gradual crescendo superimposing several
   layers of texture, and building up to a climax in
   which the opening theme appears augmented in
   the trombones and the tubas
5 Final appearance of the cornet's theme
6 Repeat of the beginning (with alterations in
   orchestration) converging on a single note (D)
   and disappearing in a flash.

Piano Sonata

22 minutes
Composed: Paris, October 1977 to February 1978
First performance: Paris, Maison de Radio France,
18 May 1978, George Benjamin (piano)
Dedication: 'To Peter Gellhorn, with affection'
Score 0 571 50578 3 on sale

This piano sonata, my first published work, was
written from October 1977 to February 1978 in
Paris during my studies at the Conservatoire with
Oliver Messiaen for composition and his wife
Yvonne Loriod for piano. At that time I wrote the
following programme note:
  'Written in three continuous movements, this
sonata employs the contrasting registers of the

piano, its resonance, and its precision and range of attack. One theme is developed throughout the work.

The first movement begins with the hesitating formation of the theme, building from one single note (E) into an energetic toccata. A slower tempo intercedes and the melodic line is calmly stated and developed. The music moves towards the bass of the piano and emerges as a mass of violent semiquavers, culminating in an explosion after which the theme disintegrates away into stacatto fragments.

The second movement (Lento) starts with a long succession of dark chords interspersed with irregular beats on a low pedal note. A brighter, more melodic section follows and prevails before the inevitable return of the opening atmosphere, which ultimately dies away.

A long trill leads to the last movement. The music erupts in a strong, percussive mood and, despite the occasional lull, advances towards a savage climax. After a brief silence, a final toccata is formed very gradually, and leads (from a deep *pp* to a sparkling *ff*) to a triumphant conclusion.'

Octet

10 minutes
Flute, clarinet, celesta, percussion, violin, viola, cello, double bass
Composed: autumn 1978, Cambridge
Commissioned by Francis Routh for the Redcliffe Concerts of British Music
First performance: London, Purcell Room, 24 February 1979, Redcliffe Ensemble, Edwin Roxburgh (conductor)
Dedication: 'For my father'
Study score 0 571 50808 1 on sale, parts for hire

This work was written in 1978 and dedicated to

my father for his sixtieth birthday. It is basically a playful scherzo, which occasionally breaks into violence or subsides into tranquillity.

The music begins tentatively with statements of most of the main material – a soft clarinet, unison chords, cello melodies, and so on. Gradually the sense of movement increases and heads towards a climax which, however, is cut short by the calmest movement of the work: a sustained, ethereal piccolo solo. The fast tempo returns and this time builds relentlessly to a full climax, after which the piece disappears with echoes of previous sounds and ultimately evaporates.

Flight

8 minutes
Solo flute
Composed: December 1978 to March 1979
First performance: Paris, Maison de Radio France,
21 March 1980, David Lodéon (flute)
Score 0 571 50596 1 on sale

This piece was inspired by the sight of birds soaring and dipping over the peaks of the Swiss Alps. Equally important to me at the time, however, was the challenge to produce clear, dramatic structure and harmony within a monody restricted to the flute's three-octave compass.

Ringed by the Flat Horizon

20 minutes
Orchestra (3 flutes, 2 oboes, cor anglais, 3 clarinets, 2 bassoons, contrabassoon, 4 horns, 3 trumpets, 3 trombones, tuba, percussion (5 players), celesta, piano, harp, strings (recommended 16.16.12.10.8))
Composed: March 1979 to January 1980

Written for the Cambridge University Musical
Society
First performance: Cambridge, 5 March 1980,
Cambridge University Musical Society Orchestra,
Mark Elder (conductor)
Dedicated to Olivier Messiaen
Full score 0 571 51078 7 on sale, parts for hire

A dramatic photograph of a thunderstorm over the
New Mexico desert and part of T. S. Eliot's *The
Waste Land* provided the inspiration for the piece.

I wanted to portray an eerie tension as the landscape is overwhelmed by a vast storm. The work
starts slowly and mysteriously, with a succession
of three textures that recur throughout the structure – weird, soft bell chords, a sustained semitone
clash, and deep tremors in the lower registers of
the orchestra which depict distant thunder.
Piccolo solos surrounded by high violins follow,
and fuller developments of the opening ideas gradually transform the momentum to faster music.

Here a sonority of wind and muted trumpets,
punctuated by wooden percussion, is juxtaposed
with quieter, more lyrical cello solos. These build
with increasing intensity, culminating in a massive
climax, after which the music slowly descends to
the bass register, subsiding in a solitary bass drum
roll.

There follows a sequence of dark, ominous
chords for full orchestra (a sound completely new
to the piece), interspersed with solo melodic lines
over the deep tremors of the opening. For a
moment the original semitone clash hovers
motionless in the air; the thunder at last erupts in
a violent explosion; and the work returns to a
mood of unreal calm, ending as it began, with a
soft bell chord.

Duo for Cello and Piano

16 minutes
Composed: April to October 1980
First performance: New York, Carnegie Recital
Hall, 5 November 1980, Ross Pople (cello),
George Benjamin (piano)

The Duo is in two strongly contrasted movements.
The first is above all energetic and climactic, char-
acterized by violent gestures in both instruments,
intertwined surging melodic lines, vehement piano
flourishes and trills, and menacing dark chords
marked by cello double stops. The second, on the
other hand, is much gentler in spirit and colour:
lyrical, unaccompanied cello solos, expressive dia-
logues between the two instruments, an eerie
melody in cello harmonics and a playful pizzicato
interlude.

In the first movement there is one brief, quiet
respite, when material from the second movement
surfaces. Similarly, the calm of the second movement is shattered by a kaleidoscope review of
material from the first movement. At its highest
point, however, the impetuous flourishes in the
piano suddenly subside, and then music from both
movements unites and gradually builds to bring
the work to a serene and radiant conclusion.

A Mind of Winter

10 minutes
Text: 'The Snow Man' by Wallace Stevens
Soprano and orchestra (2 flutes, oboe, cor anglais,
2 clarinets, 2 bassoons, 2 horns, 2 trumpets, per-
cussion (1 player), strings (6.6.4.4.2))
Composed: November 1980 to May 1981
Written for the Scottish Chamber Orchestra and
the Aldeburgh Festival

First performance: Snape Maltings, 26 June 1981,
Teresa Cahill (soprano), Scottish Chamber
Orchestra, Jerzy Maksymiuk (conductor)
Dedication: 'To my mother on her birthday'
Full score o 571 50718 2 on sale, parts for hire

A Mind of Winter is a setting of 'The Snow Man',
by the American poet, Wallace Stevens. A contemporary of Eliot and Pound, he lived most of
his life in New England, and it is only relatively
recently that his true stature has been widely
acknowledged.

Two things immediately appealed to me about
'The Snow Man' – the abundance of beautiful winter imagery within its compact frame, and the deep
ambiguity of its meaning. In this setting, the
frozen, snow-covered terrain is depicted by an
immobile four-part A-minor chord on muted
strings; suspended cymbals and multidivided string
glissandi portray icy gusts of wind. Various aspects
of the scene are suggested by other instruments – a
solo oboe, woodwind in groups of two or three
players, two lyrical horns. At the centre of the
landscape stands the solitary Snow Man – a muted
piccolo trumpet – around whom the soprano
weaves slow, angular phrases whilst beholding,
'Nothing that is not there and the nothing that is.'

The Snow Man
One must have a mind of winter
To regard the frost and the boughs
Of the pine-trees crusted with snow;

And have been cold a long time
To behold the junipers shagged with ice,
The spruces rough in the distant glitter

Of the January sun; and not to think
Of any misery in the sound of the wind,
In the sound of a few leaves,

Which is the sound of the land
Full of the same wind
That is blowing in the same bare place

For the listener, who listens in the snow,
And, nothing himself, beholds
Nothing that is not there and the nothing that is.

Sortilèges

11 minutes
Solo piano
Commissioned by Paul Crossley with funds provided by Northern Arts
Composed: July to October 1981
First performance: Cheltenham International
Festival, 15 July 1982, Paul Crossley (piano)
Dedicated to Yvonne Loriod
Score 0 571 50671 2 on sale

This title was chosen because the piece inhabits a
musical world of fantasy, with a wide range of
contrasts in harmonic colour, register and velocity.

The first of two movements serves as a slow
introduction. It sets the scene with ominous
chords spread throughout the whole keyboard,
enclosing a sudden premonition of future material.

The second movement erupts with explosive
gestures, galloping bass semiquavers and dynamic
flourishes. These daemonic sounds are contrasted
with *cantabile* phrases and an incantatory
scherzando. Tension builds as all this material
combines and verges on pandemonium at which
point the movement dissolves into waves of *pppp*
semiquavers.

After a pause, the gentler side of the piece is at
last allowed to sing and predominate, and the work
appears to be approaching a tranquil conclusion –
but there is one remaining spell, for the very end.

At First Light

22 minutes
Chamber orchestra of fourteen players (flute,
oboe, clarinet (doubling bass clarinet), bassoon
(doubling contrabassoon), horn, trumpet, trom-
bone, percussion, piano (doubling celesta), 2 vio-
lins, viola, cello, double bass)
Commissioned by the London Sinfonietta with
funds provided by the Arts Council of Great
Britain
Composed: January to October 1982
First performance: London, St John's, Smith
Square, 23 November 1982, London Sinfonietta,
Simon Rattle (conductor)
Dedicated to Donald and Kathleen Mitchell
Full score 0 571 50718 2 on sale, parts for hire

In the Tate Gallery there is a late Turner oil painting, *Norham Castle, Sunrise*. The twelfth-century
castle in this picture is silhouetted against a huge,
golden sun. What struck me immediately about
this beautiful image was the way in which solid
objects – fields, cows, and the castle itself – appear
virtually to have melted under the intense sunlight.
It is as if the paint were still wet.

Abstractly, this observation has been very
important to the way I have composed the piece.
A 'solid object' can be formed as a punctuated,
clearly defined musical phrase. This can be
'melted' into a flowing, nebulous continuum of
sound. There can be all manner of transformations and interactions between these two ways of
writing.

Equally important, however, this piece is a contemplation of dawn, a celebration of the colours and noises of daybreak. It is set in three movements: in the short, opening one, superimposed fanfares burst into hazy, undefined textures. After a pause, the extended second movement follows, itself divided into several contrasted sections, full of abrupt changes in mood and tension. The concluding movement arrives without a break, and progresses in a continuous, flowing line illuminated with ever more resonant harmonies.

Fanfare for Aquarius

40 seconds
Chamber orchestra of fifteen players (flute, oboe, clarinet, bassoon, horn, trumpet, trombone, percussion, piano, harp, 2 violins, viola, cello, double bass)
Composed: October 1983
Written for the first concert by the Aquarius ensemble
First performance: London, Queen Elizabeth Hall, 18 October 1983, Aquarius, Nicholas Cleobury (conductor)
Full score and parts for hire

A very short, pugnacious fanfare for ensemble, based around the note middle C.

Three Studies for Solo Piano

18 minutes
First complete performance: London, Queen Elizabeth Hall, 4 February 1986, George Benjamin (piano)

1. *Fantasy on Iambic Rhythm*
    11 minutes

Composed: December 1984 to April 1985
First performance: London, Queen Elizabeth Hall,
4 February 1986, George Benjamin (piano)
Dedication: 'For my sister, Laura'
Score 0 571 50948 7 on sale

2. *Meditation on Haydn's Name*
3 minutes
Composed: December 1981 to January 1982
First performance: London, BBC Radio 3, 31
March 1982, John McCabe (piano)
Dedicated to Sarah Taylor
Score 0 571 50848 0 on sale

3. *Relativity Rag*
4 minutes
Composed: October to November 1984
First performance: Cardiff, University College,
23 November 1984, George Benjamin (piano)
Dedicated to Robin Holloway
Score 0 571 50848 0 on sale

The first and longest of these three studies, the
Fantasy, takes iambic rhythm (short–long) as its
starting point. Various contrasted types of music
evolve from this rhythmic 'cell', and are transformed and juxtaposed thoughout a wide range of
moods, often at great speed. A slow, gentle melody
interrupts at a climactic moment and spreads reso-
nantly across the complete range of the piano,
before the final build towards a jubilant conclusion.

Meditation on Haydn's Name was commissioned by the BBC in 1982 to commemorate the
250th anniversary of Haydn's birth. The individual letters of Haydn's name can easily find equiva-
lents in musical notes and the result is a five-note
phrase – BADDG. These notes sound as a chord,
hovering in the centre of the texture throughout
this piece, around which lyrical lines of a similar

harmonic colour diverge and resolve.

Relativity Rag begins with a simple two-section
Rag-Time. As it progresses, however, things begin
to change – phrases are cut up like bits of film, the
tempi of the hands separate, the harmony distorts
and eventually the Rag is transformed beyond
recognition. It reforms out of a dense cloud of
sound towards the end, and briefly flourishes
before being finally crushed and sent spinning off
the top of the keyboard.

Jubilation

10 minutes
Orchestra (3 flutes, 2 oboes, cor anglais, 2 clarinets, bass clarinet, 2 bassoons, contrabassoon, 4
horns, 3 trumpets, 3 trombones, percussion (4
players), piano, synthesizer, harp, violins (divided
in three groups, minimum: 8.8.8), violas, cellos,
double basses; and mixed children's group: 20
recorders, 4 horns, 4 trumpets, 4 trombones, 7
steel drums, percussion (minimum 10 players),
choir of 100 children's voices)
Commissioned by the Inner London Education
Authority with funds provided by them and the
Arts Council of Great Britain
Composed: May to August 1985
First performance: London, Royal Festival Hall,
16 September 1985, London Schools Symphony
Orchestra, George Benjamin (conductor)
Dedicated to John Hyman
Full score 0 571 51005 1 on sale, parts for hire

The forces used in this short work are enormous.
The atmosphere of the piece, however, is above all
one of meditation, and the vast forces are
employed rather as a wide palette of instrumental
colour than for massed effects.

The piece progresses as a processional, setting

off in darkness with percussive pulses and swooping synthesizer glissandi. One by one the extra groups of players enter – the steel drums acting as a 'gamelan', the chorus chanting *sol–fa*, virtuoso recorder flourishes and antiphonal brass calls. As the instrumental forces accumulate, the piece builds towards a radiant conclusion.

Panorama

3 minutes
Tape, realized at IRCAM
Composed: November 1985
Tape for hire

Written as a study for *Antara*, this short computer-music piece consists of one of the oldest and simplest of musical sounds – panpipes. At first appearing in a simple modal melody, they are soon transformed into an imaginary world of gigantic panpipes, tiny whistles, percussive rhythms and shooting glissandi.

Antara

20 minutes
Ensemble of sixteen instrumentalists: 2 flutes, 2 computerized keyboards, 2 trombones, percussion (2 players), 3 violins, 2 violas, 2 cellos, double bass, synthesizer
Piece realized at IRCAM. Musical assistants: Thierry Lancino and Cort Lippe
Commissioned by IRCAM for the tenth anniversary of the Centre Georges-Pompidou
Composed: October 1985 to March 1987
First performance: Paris, IRCAM, 25 April 1987, Sophie Cherrier, Céline Nessi (flutes), Pierre-Laurent Aimard, Ichiro Nodaïra (keyboards), Ensemble Intercontemporain, George Benjamin (conductor)

Dedicated to Tristan and Françoise Murail
Full score 0 571 51071 X on sale, parts for hire

During the summer of 1984 I attended the six-
week educational course at IRCAM. Whenever I
left the Institute I found the square in front of the
Pompidou Centre ringing with the sound of panpipes. A South American group would busk there
every day, playing their traditional music, and it
was striking to see that huge, metallic building
completely dominated by these little bamboo
tubes.

Antara is an ancient Inca word for panpipe, a
term still used today in Peru. And the history of
the panpipes is indeed ancient, with roots dating
back thousands of years around the world, not
only in South America, but also China, the Pacific
and Southern Europe. There is an equally large
variety of panpipes still in existence today, ranging
from big single tubes to rows of small whistles.

Panpipes have many qualities which have been
lost to today's concert instruments, among them a
vibrant rawness and freshness of timbre.
However, panpipes also have many severe constraints, including great limitations on pitch
mobility and velocity. Long-held notes are impossible, as are large chords. Even some melodic lines
cause considerable difficulty as, on larger tubes,
they have to be shared between two or more players (a technique akin to 'hocketing' in medieval
music). The computer can solve all these problems and more, and so in this piece the sound of
the oldest of all wind instruments has been
recorded and transferred to the most modern of
computers, initially the IRCAM 4X, creating an
instrument ranging from the equivalent of panpipes 20 metres high to pipes of only a few mil-
limetres. These are played via two Yamaha

keyboards, which are surrounded by an ensemble of fourteen players.

At first the panpipes are used entirely melodically, almost naturally, and they encounter and communicate with two modern flutes. The flutes themselves often play in a manner akin to their ancient predecessors, hocketing melodies from left to right with almost no vibrato and a breathy sonority. (Only later in the piece does the playing style of the modern flute begin to evolve.) Eight strings act as a background to these confrontations, often in the form of a dance-like accompaniment.

This active, energetic music is threatened by two deep, growling trombones and two percussionists, the latter playing almost exclusively on a plethora of anvils. These forces invoke the real power of the computerized keyboards – huge, sustained microtonal chords, sweeping glissandi, breath-like sounds, percussive timbres – all derived from the original panpipes. At the largest climax the keyboards engulf the orchestral anvils in a myriad of metallic sound, after which the opposed sound sources of metal and reed fuse, and speed towards a coruscating but tranquil conclusion.

In this piece, the electronic part is played live on the keyboards, with no tape, no click-track and no electronic effects. This not only allows spontaneity, but also permits a deeper integration in compositional terms between the electronic and the acoustic.

Upon Silence

10 mins
Text: 'The Long-Legged Fly' by W. B. Yeats
Dedication: 'In memory of Michael Vyner (1943–89)'
Original version for mezzo-soprano and five viols: 1 treble viol, 2 tenor viols, 2 bass viols

Composed: 15 February to 22 September 1990
Written for Fretwork
First performance: London, Queen Elizabeth Hall,
30 October 1990, Susan Bickley (mezzo-soprano)
and Fretwork, George Benjamin (conductor)
Viol version score 0 571 51251 8 on sale

Revised version for mezzo-soprano and group of
seven strings: 2 violas, 3 cellos, 2 double basses
Commissioned by the Opéra de Paris, Bastille
Composed: San Francisco, August 1991
First performance: Paris, amphitheatre of the
Opéra-Bastille, 21 March 1992, Susan Bickley
(mezzo-soprano) and Musique Oblique, George
Benjamin (conductor)
Score 0 571 51251 8 on sale, parts for hire

'The Long-Legged Fly', a late Yeats poem, portrays three momentous figures in history absorbed
in silent contemplation: Julius Caesar planning a
crucial military campaign, Helen of Troy as an
adolescent in Sparta and Michelangelo painting
the Sistine Chapel.

The verses are set in a syllabic manner, while
each successive chorus is set to increasingly
lengthy melismas, like the long-legged fly above
the water, the voice hovers above the viols' now
turbulent, now still stream of sound.

I have treated the viols as a new family of string
instruments – three sizes, all with six strings and
frets, capable of an array of hitherto unexplored
techniques and sonorities. Amongst these I might
mention the almost complete absence of vibrato,
the novel bowing technique, the potential for
numerous natural harmonics, super-fast tremoli
and resonant pizzicati.

Long-Legged Fly
That civilisation may not sink
Its great battle lost,

Quiet the dog, tether the pony
To a distant post;
Our master Caesar is in the tent
Where the maps are spread;
His eyes fixed upon nothing,
A hand under his head.

Like a long-legged fly upon the stream
His mind moves upon silence.

That the topless towers be burnt
And men recall that face,
Move most gently if move you must
In this lonely place.
She thinks, part woman, three parts child,
That nobody looks; her feet
Practise a tinker shuffle
Picked up on a street.

Like a long-legged fly upon the stream
Her mind moves upon silence.

That girls at puberty may find
The first Adam in their thought,
Shut the door of the Pope's chapel,
Keep those children out.
There on that scaffolding reclines
Michael Angelo.
With no more sound than the mice make
His hand moves to and fro.

Like a long-legged fly upon the stream
His mind moves upon silence.

Sudden Time

15 minutes
Orchestra (4 flutes, 2 oboes, cor anglais, 2 clar-

inets, bass clarinet, 2 bassoons, contrabassoon, 4
horns, 4 trumpets, 4 trombones, tuba, timpani,
percussion (5 players), upright piano, 2 harps,
strings (14.12.10.8.6))
Composed: 1989 to July 1993
First performance: London, Queen Elizabeth Hall,
21 July 1993 (Meltdown Festival), London
Philharmonic Orchestra, George Benjamin (conductor)
Dedicated to Isaiah Berlin
Score 0 571 51578 9 on sale, parts for hire

The gestation period for this orchestral piece was
lengthy – the first sketches date back to 1983 and
the last bars were completed shortly before the
première a decade later. As this period progressed
my ideas for the type of piece I wanted to write
gradually crystallized – this process involved the
invention of a new technical approach as well as
the rejection of certain concepts tied to my earlier
works.

Above all I wanted the music to flow with considerable agility, the material evolving across the
orchestra, sometimes in several different directions
simultaneously. To achieve this the texture
throughout is conceived in linear terms, the audible harmony being created by the fusion of separate lines.

The resulting structure oscillates between
focused, pulsed simplicity and whirlpools of complex polyrhythm. An organic sense of continuity
between these extremes is made possible by the
fact that all material, however plain or elaborate,
is based on a few musical cells of great simplicity.

Sudden Time basically divides into two continuous movements, the first (lasting about five minutes) acting as a turbulent introduction to the
second, where a subliminal metre is perpetually
distorted and then reassembled.

Even though an exceptionally large orchestra is employed, my intention at times was to achieve a transparency akin to chamber music. Material was directly conceived into full score and there is virtually no decorative padding or conventional doubling. Some unusual instruments are employed, including a quartet of alto flutes, a pair of miniature recorders, a muted piano and a plethora of mini-tablas which accompany the extremely difficult viola solo at the work's end.

The title is a quotation from Wallace Stevens's poem, 'Martial Cadenza': 'It was like sudden time in a world without time.' Some of the concepts behind the piece can be illustrated by a dream I once had in which the sound of a thunderclap seemed to stretch to at least a minute's duration before suddenly circulating, as if in a spiral, through my head. I then woke, and realized that I was in fact experiencing merely the first second of a thunderclap. I had perceived it in dream-time, in between and in real time.

Although this is but an analogy, a sense of elasticity, of things stretching, warping and then coalescing, is something that I have tried to capture in this piece.

Three Inventions for Chamber Orchestra

17 minutes

Chamber orchestra of 24 players (2 flutes (doubling piccolos and alto flute), oboe (doubling cor anglais), 3 clarinets (2 doubling bass clarinets and l contrabass clarinet), bassoon (doubling contrabassoon), 2 horns, trumpet (doubling piccolo, trumpet and flugelhorn), trombone (doubling euphonium), percussion (2 players), piano (doubling celesta), 3 violins (1 doubling viola), 2 violas, 2 cellos, 2 double basses)

Commissioned by Betty Freeman for the 75th Salzburg Festival
First performance: Salzburg, Mozarteum, 27 July 1995, Ensemble Modern, George Benjamin (conductor)
Full score 0 571 517902 1 on sale, parts for hire

1st Invention (originally entitled *Tribute*)
4 minutes
Completed: 26 November 1993
First performance: London, Barbican Hall, 29 November 1993, London Sinfonietta, Kent Nagano (conductor)
Dedication: 'In memory of Olivier Messiaen'

2nd Invention
3 minutes
Completed: 19 July 1995

3rd Invention
10 minutes
Completed: 11 July 1995
Dedicated to Alexander Goehr

Three movements, deliberately contrasted in their form and colour, written for twenty-four players.

The first Invention is mainly serene and luminous in atmosphere. A brief introduction leads to a sustained flugel-horn solo whose melodic curves create constantly transforming harmonic implications.

The second Invention is fast, loud and rhythmic. A virtuoso cor anglais solo announces what appears to be a conventional triple metre; however, within a very brief time all manner of irregular figuration and unexpected tempo juxtapositions contort this metre beyond recognition. Half-way through, the texture launches into an energetic tutti; only at the very end is metrical regularity reinstated by an acrobatic clarinet solo.

The final Invention mirrors the first in technical conception, but the tone is radically different. Antiphonal tuned gongs and bass drums surround a network of materials which weave through the whole ensemble: slow bass octaves, floating consonant harmonies, rushing filigree scales. As these materials rotate across the structure in ever-changing combinations, they encounter a variety of foreground melodic solos: initially a serpentine contrabassoon, later a menacing euphonium and more florid violins and violas. As the movement progresses, harmony and rhythm mutate into constantly new territory, but the heavy, bass-dominated pulse, which underpins the texture, remains remorselessly regular until the very end.

Sometime Voices

9 minutes
Baritone, Chorus and Orchestra
Completed September 1996
Commissioned for the opening concerts of the
Bridgewater Hall, Manchester, by the Hallé
Orchestra with funds from the Arts Council of
England and Royal Mail
Orchestra (3 flutes, 3 oboes, 3 clarinets, 2 bassoons, contrabassoon, 4 horns, 3 trumpets, 3 trombones, tuba, timpani, percussion (4 players), celesta, 2 harps, mandolin, banjo, strings)
First performance: Manchester, Bridgewater Hall,
11 September 1996, Hallé Orchestra and Chorus,
William Dazeley (baritone), Kent Nagano (conductor)
Dedicated to Kent Nagano
Full score and parts for hire

Rather than a conventional fanfare for the opening of Manchester's Bridgewater Hall, this mostly transparent and quiet piece explored Caliban's famous speech in Act 3, Scene 2 of *The Tempest*, in which he describes a magical music pervading the island on which he lives:

'Sometimes a thousand twangling instruments
Will hum about mine ears; and sometime voices,
That if I then had waked after long sleep,
Will make me sleep again, and then in dreaming
The clouds methought would open and show riches
Ready to drop upon me, that when I waked
I cried to dream again.'

The savage Caliban sings in long, forceful phrases whilst the orchestra drifts between an eerie tranquillity and mercurial activity. Behind this, the chorus, acting as spirits – sometimes benign, sometimes menacing – invoke his name.

Viola, Viola

9 minutes
Viola duo
Completed: July 1997
First performance: Tokyo Opera City Concert Hall, 16 September 1997
Yuri Bashmet, Nobuko Imai
Dedicated to Michael Waldman

Viola, Viola was commissioned by the Tokyo Opera City Cultural Foundation of which the Artistic Director was Toru Takemitsu, for the opening of the Tokyo Opera City Concert Hall on 16 September 1997. I was naturally eager to respond to this proposal from my late much-lamented friend Toru Takemitsu. The idea of a viola duo for his friends Yuri Bashmet and Nobuko Imai was entirely his. My initial thoughts of how to solve the many compositional problems inherent within this most unconventional medium may have suggested the viola's accustomed role as

Viola, Viola (extract). © 1997 Faber Music Ltd.
Reproduced by kind permission.

a melancholy voice hidden in the shadows. However, once under way, a completely different instrumental character – fiery and energetic – imposed itself.

My desire at times was to conjure an almost orchestral depth and variety in sound. This accounts for the fact that the two viola parts are virtually braided together – indeed, clearly independent lines only begin to flower towards the work's *cantabile* centre. The implied harmony is intended to be as sonorous as possible, the texture sometimes maintaining four or more parts for sustained periods.

Transcription

Fantasia VII (Purcell, arranged Benjamin)
Clarinet, violin, cello, celesta
Completed: June 1995
First performance: Aldeburgh Festival, 16 June 1995
George Pieterson, clarinet; Vera Beths, violin;
Anner Bylsma, cello; Reinbert de Leeuw, celesta.

This transcription for violin, cello, clarinet and celesta was written for the 1995 Aldeburgh Festival, to commemorate the 300th anniversary of Purcell's death.

The works of George Benjamin are published by:
Faber Music Limited
3 Queen Square
London WC1N 3AU
Tel: +44 171 833 7911/2
Fax: +44 171 833 7939
E-mail: promotion@fabermusic.co.uk
website: www.fabermusic.co.uk

Discography

At First Light – A Mind of Winter –
Ringed by the Flat Horizon

> London Sinfonietta. Conductor: George Benjamin.
> BBC Symphony Orchestra. Conductor: Mark Elder.
> *Nimbus Records – NI5075*, 1987

Antara

> London Sinfonietta. Conductor: George Benjamin.
> (With works by Pierre Boulez, Jonathan Harvey.)
> *Nimbus – NI 5167*, 1989

At First Light

> Le Nouvel Ensemble Moderne. Conductor:
> Lorraine Vaillancourt. (With works by Ada
> Gentile, Kaija Saariaho, György Ligeti.)
> *UMMUS – UMM 102*, 1990

Flight

> Irmela Nolte, flute. (With works by Giacinto Scelsi,
> Goffredo Petrassi, Christobal Halffter)
> *Blackbird Records – MP 1001*, 1990

Piano Sonata

> George Benjamin, piano.
> *Nimbus Records – NI 1415*, 1991

Panorama

Musical Machinery UP04MM, 1994

At First Light

Tokyo Sinfonietta. Conductor: Kunitaka Kokaji.
(With works by Magnus Lindberg, Gérard Grisey,
Iannis Xenakis.)
TS 95001, 1995

Flight

Ingrid Culliford, flute. (With works by York
Bowen, Roberto Gerhard, Elizabeth Maconchy,
William Alwyn.)
Loret LNT 107, 1995

Sudden Time

London Philharmonic Orchestra. Conductor:
George Benjamin.
Nimbus Records – NI 1432, 1994

Sudden Time – Three Inventions for Chamber Orchestra – Octet – Upon Silence (two versions)

Susan Bickley, mezzo-soprano. London
Philharmonic Orchestra, London Sinfonietta,
Fretwork. Conductor: George Benjamin.
Nimbus Records – NI 5505

Bibliography

Texts by George Benjamin

'La paternité contestée' (on Boulez), in *Eclats/Boulez*. Texts assembled by Claude Samuel. Editions du Centre Georges-Pompidou, 1986.

'Quelques réflexions sur le son musical', in *Le timbre, métaphore pour la composition*. Texts assembled and introduced by Jean-Baptiste Barrière. Christian Bourgois éditeur, IRCAM, Centre Georges-Pompidou, 1991.

'Pelléas and the confrontation with convention' (on Debussy's opera), in the opera programme, Welsh National Opera (Cardiff), 1992.

'Glorious legacy of a humble church organist' (nécrologie de Messiaen), in the *Observer*, 3 May 1992. Reprinted in French, 'Le maître des maîtres', in *Le Monde de la musique* no. 156, June 1992, and in German, 'Der Meister der Meister', in *Musik-Texte* no. 45, July 1992.

'Puccini's Turandot in Lyon', in Japanese, in *Ikebana sogetsu*, no. 203, August 1992.

'Questionnaire' in the IRCAM programme, Centre Georges-Pompidou, September 1992.

'*Sudden Time*, 1993', in the Meltdown Festival programme, South Bank Centre, London, July 1993. In French: in the programme of the concerts for the 10th anniversary of the Lyon Opera Orchestra, 3–4 October 1993.

'Comme une coulée de lave' (on Tristan Murail), in the Ars Musica festival programme book, Brussels, 1994.

'Last Dance' (on Ravel's *La Valse*), in *The Musical Times*, July 1994.

'The Master of Harmony', in *The Messiaen Companion*. Faber & Faber, 1995.

Texts on individual works by Debussy, Ravel, Stravinsky, etc. linked to BBC Radio 3's 'Sounding the Century', *BBC Music* magazine, 1997–99.

Text on Janáček, for the *Sunday Times*, 1997.

Text on Sibelius, for the UK Sibelius Society's International Seminar, 1997.

Texts on George Benjamin

Andrew Clements: 'George Benjamin', in the *Financial Times*, 7 March 1980

Brigitte Schiffer: 'George Benjamin's *Ringed by the Flat Horizon*', in *Tempo* nos. 133/134, September 1980.

Arnold Whittall: '*A Mind of Winter, Sortilèges*', in *Music and Letters*, 1984.

Andrew Porter: 'Profile', in the *New Yorker*, 5 March 1984.

'George Benjamin', in *New Sounds, New Personalities*. British Composers of the 1980s in conversation with Paul Griffiths. Faber & Faber, 1985.

Nicholas Kenyon: 'First Light', in *The Listener*, 21 March 1985.

Paul Driver: 'The composer with the Turner

touch', in the *Sunday Times*, 3 August 1986.

Peter Heyworth: 'A brilliant start sustained', in the *Observer*, 3 August 1986.

Ivanka Stoianova: 'La solitude des inventeurs de son', in *Le Monde de la musique*, November 1987.

Malcolm Hayes: 'Synthesizers and panpipes', in the *Sunday Telegraph*, 14 May 1989.

Paul Fisher: 'Shedding light on heavy music', in *Classic CD*, June 1990.

Alan Rusbridger: 'Prodigy in search of a voice', the *Guardian*, 29 October 1990.

Wanda Dobrovská: 'Chci zkusit tolik věcí, kolik je možno' (in Czech), in *Hudební rozhledy*, no. 44, 1991.

E. Baumgartner: 'Musik die wie dans Leben ist', in *Wiener Zeitung*, 24 March 1991.

Ana Maria Dávila: 'George Benjamin presenta su propria obra en el Lliure', in *El Observador* (Barcelona), 3 May 1991.

James Weir: 'George Benjamin', in *Contemporary Composers*. St James Press, 1992.

Christian Leblé: 'Musiciens de Notre Temps' (chapter on George Benjamin), Editions Plume et SACEM, 1992.

Lidia Bramani: 'George Benjamin' (in Italian), in the Ricordi catalogue (Milan), July 1992.

Frieda Verdonk: 'George Benjamin, I presume?' (in Flemish), in *De Standaard*, 16 September 1993.

Robert Jan Haitink: 'De muzikale tidj' (in Dutch), in *Entr'acte*, November 1993.

Jacques Michon: 'Entretien avec George Benjamin', in *L'Education musicale* no. 413, December 1994.

Francesco Leprino: 'Conversazione con George Benjamin' (in Italian), in *Ricordi oggi*, December 1994.

Entry on George Benjamin, in *Rough Guide to Classical Music on CD*, 1994.

Christian Leblé: 'Le Benjamin de Salzbourg', in *Libération*, 1 August 1995.

Michelangelo Zurletti: 'Benjamin dice addio a suo padre Messiaen', in *La Repubblica*, 5 August 1995.

David Bruce: 'The Tongue Free' (on *Three Inventions*), in *The Musical Times*, November 1995.

Andrew Clements: 'Throwing off the Messiaen complex', in the *Guardian*, 17 November 1995.

Daniel Robellaz: 'Archipel invite George Benjamin, compositeur actuel très en vue', in *La Tribune de Genève,* 2 March 1996.

Erik Voermans: 'Benjamin lijdt niet aan millennium-blues' (in Dutch), in *Het Parol*, 21 March 1996.

José Antonio Canton: 'George Benjamin, compositor – la belleza de la Alhambra enamora al músico', in *La Cronica* (Grenada), 28 April 1996.

John Whitley: 'Tuning in to the 20th Century', in the *Daily Telegraph*, 17 February 1997.

France de Kinder: 'La Musique comme expression d'une volonté intérieure', Ars Musica festival brochure, March 1997, Brussels.